# The Forgotten Faith

## The Witness of the Celtic Saints

*Anthony Duncan*

SKYLIGHT PRESS

This edition published in Great Britain in 2013 by Skylight Press, 210 Brooklyn Road, Cheltenham, Glos GL51 8EA

First published in 2002 by Sun Chalice Books, Oceanside, USA.

Designed and typeset by Rebsie Fairholm
Publisher: Daniel Staniforth

**www.skylightpress.co.uk**

Printed and bound in Great Britain by Lightning Source, Milton Keynes. Typeset in Vulpa, a font by Schizotype. Titles set in Luminari, a font by Canada Type, and Kereru by Daniel Reeve.

British Library Cataloguing in Publication Data.
A catalogue record for this book is available from the British Library.

ISBN 978-1-908011-71-8

**St Kentigern baptising Merlin: stained glass window in Stobo Kirk, Scottish Borders.**

# Contents

*chapter one*

# Saints, Sites and Ourselves

*A thin place this,*
*Where treads my foot more silently;*
*There is a magic here*
*Which makes that dark and nail-studded door*
*That locks dimension from my consciousness*
*Lean on its bolts in a sudden breeze*
*And stir my vapid air.*
*There is a thinness in this place,*
*Translucent to my senses;*
*Sensing I know not what*
*Save that I'm conscious of my hair*
*And that I breathe, that I can hear*
*The sound that silence makes*
*And know a warmth about my face;*
*And that I walk more slowly home.*

THERE ARE TIMES in all our lives when we discover that we are in 'a thin place,' a place that causes all the noise within us to be still and enables us, all unexpectedly, to "hear the sound that silence makes." Something has been said to the very depths of us; we don't know what it is that our spirit has heard but we "walk more slowly home" as the result of the hearing of it.

More often than not these are places such as T.S.Eliot once described, "Where prayer has been valid." In other words where there has been an association of people with place and, in some strange way, a consecration of both which transcends the passage of time for it is, by its very nature, timeless. No man lives for himself, neither does any woman. It is a Christian belief – more often forgotten than called to mind – that there is but one creature – Humanity – and you and I and everybody else, past, present and to come, are all "persons" of that one creature. As the New Testament reminds us, "we are members, one of another." This is why we are given pause, usually unexpectedly, by holy places where prayer has been valid; there is a common, human sharing in the mystery of Love and of ultimate meaning and we have, for a brief moment, experienced something of it.

# The Experience of Exile

The poet Kathleen Raine once described the Scottish Highlands to me as "an image of that from which I am an exile." There is an exile in all of us for, as we are reminded by all manner of Biblical imagery and mythology, we are to some extent 'strangers,' 'sojourners,' and here, 'we have no continuing city.' Life is a journey; in other words it is dynamic and not static, and there is a longing for 'home' in all of us, however sophisticated we may think ourselves to be. The Celtic lands are, for a multitude of folk world-wide, images of that 'home' from which we are exile. These are not the sentimental sort of images full of tartans, or of Irish eyes smiling, but the deeply felt and only half-consciously acknowledged longings for what we may probably best describe as *roots*.

Roots have many dimensions. There is the physical dimension; this is where I come from, this is where I belong, I – or my fathers – were born here. Or, in that wonderful but untranslatable German word, this is my *heimat*. The emotional dimension follows on. Nobody is more 'English' than the Englishman abroad! There is more tartan worn in the USA than in Scotland, and more Gaelic spoken in Canada than in the Scottish *Gaidhealtachd*. One could expand at length, but the point is sufficiently made. Any group, in exile in a foreign land, clings fiercely to its identity. However strongly

8

it may have identified with its new home, at an everyday level, it is rooted in another place and let no man forget it! In World War One, in addition to the many battalions of the Northumberland Fusiliers and the Durham Light Infantry marching to war from the North East of England's Tyneside, two whole and quite separate Brigades were recruited: "The Tyneside Scottish" and "The Tyneside Irish." The very fact of it speaks volumes.

There is also the spiritual dimension to an individual's roots and this is by no means to be divorced from the physical and emotional. It does, however transcend them and it reaches out to touch other persons of the one creature. Humanity, as well as those who might claim to be more immediately – and however remotely – tribally connected.

"Where prayer has been valid," where there has been an association of consecrated lives with places, there has very often been effected, as we have said, *a consecration of both* which transcends time because it is timeless. It is at this point that we are obliged to take note of the men and women whose lives were consecrated with such abiding effects for the rest of us. These are those men and women whom we are accustomed to describe as the Celtic Saints.

# What are Saints?

We call them the Celtic Saints, but what do we mean by that? In the first place we mean those men and women of the Celtic races who have been remembered for their Christ-like character, first by generations of people local to their places of life and work, and then, formally, by the Church as a whole when the custom of formal canonisation of Saints became established. In their lifetimes they were very ordinary men and women in whom the Divine Grace worked a transformation – a transfiguration indeed which gradually became apparent to their contemporaries.

At that famous meeting between the Briton, St Kentigern and the Scots/Irish St Columba, when they exchanged their pastoral staffs as a sign of unity and brotherhood, they did not address each other thus: "Good afternoon, St Kentigern," and "Good afternoon, St Columba!" The very word *saint* needs to be examined more closely than is usually the case, for this is highly relevant to our understanding of their social context as well as their spiritual.

St Paul, in those letters of his to Christian communities which we find in the New Testament, writes "to the saints" – in Corinth, or in Rome or wherever they happened to be. He was writing to the *local Church*, and he addressed them as "the saints" because they were partakers, by faith and baptism, of the sanctity – the holiness – of the Incarnate Son of God. Their sainthood was not their own, it was the very holiness of God! We learn, in the New Testament, that "the saints" included a number of very tiresome and difficult people, just like any church congregation at any time in history. It is human nature that is gradually transfigured from within by the Divine Grace, it is not a plaster statue! The process takes time and is costly, both to the individual and to his or her companions. "The saints" have always to learn to live with each other, and they must also learn to love each other. They do not always like each other! This is as true today as it was in the earliest Centuries of the Faith.

The members of a Christian community – like the Welsh *Llan* – were often referred to as "the saints" in a strictly New Testament sense. They were Christian believers in a still widely non-Christian, or at best partially Christian society. It was only after their deaths, through remembrance of them and their qualities, that some of them began to be referred to in terms of a new and quite different meaning of the word *Saint*.

The canonised Saints are those whom the whole Church acknowledges as holy and as having manifested in their earthly lives the character of Christ. But there is more to it than this, for there was, in earlier times, a strong awareness of the closeness of Heaven to Earth and of the continuing companionship of the Christ-like – the Saints – with earthly men and women in their earthly circumstances.

Indeed the piety of the hearth knew no separation at all between the farmer, his cow, the Saints, the Mother of God and the Blessed Trinity in whom all things abide. Thus the *Cronan Bleoghan* or *Milking Song:*

*Come, Mary, and milk my cow,*
*Come, Bride, and encompass her,*
*Come, Columba the benign,*
*And twine thine arms around my cow.*
*Ho my heifer, ho my gentle heifer,*
*Ho my heifer, ho my gentle heifer,*
*Ho my heifer, ho my gentle heifer,*
*My heifer dear, generous and kind,*
*For the sake of the High King take to thy calf.*
*(Carmina Gadelica, Vol. 1, 99)*

A Christian believer lives his life, milks his cow and abides forever in the fellowship of his friends in Heaven, and all in God, and God in all. This vivid understanding shines through the whole of Celtic spirituality. It is, perhaps, this very quality of wholeness of faith, and of unity of faith with life, which the over-intellectualised Westerner is beginning to seek with something like desperation. We proclaim belief in the Communion of Saints every time we recite the Apostles' Creed, but for multitudes of Western Christians, the thing ends there. It is almost politically incorrect (in a religious sense) to then behave as if we actually *believed* it, or expected to experience the Communion of Saints as a vibrant reality in our own lives.

# The Land and its people

The Genesis myth of the brothers Cain and Abel represents, amongst other things, the conflict between two diametrically opposed views of the relationship of mankind to the rest of creation. It is, in part, a commentary upon a tension felt in Israel, both between them and their neighbours, and within themselves but it has a much wider connotation and is very relevant to our own study.

Abel, the herdsman, belongs to the land as a living, conscious and responsible part of it. He claims no ownership, for the very

11

idea of owning land is as absurd to him as the idea of owning the air he breathes. This, in Biblical terms, is the pure life of the desert, the 'wandering Aramaean,' herdsman and *dynamic partaker* rather than *static cultivator* and would-be-owner of that which can only belong to God. Cain is the farmer, the exploiter, the keeper-out of trespassers, the rival, the man who is his own little god, the uneasy conscience which – as always – kills that which makes it uneasy. There is, after all, nobody in any generation for a man to kill except his own brother.

The Celt of the Age of the Saints, like the Red Indian and the Australian Aborigine, to name but a few others like him, represented Abel. The idea of land ownership, in any sense that we now know it, was quite foreign. Cain came later, murderously as always, in the form of Tudor and Stuart 'plantations' in Ireland, foreign invasions and feudal landlord systems introduced into, or imposed upon, Wales and Scotland. We need not presently concern ourselves with these things other than to note the very different social context of those earlier centuries, particularly where the Roman Empire had hardly touched or had not touched at all.

To the early Celtic Christian, the landscape was not only beautiful, its beauty was the beauty of its Creator for it was holy. Creation is an icon of its Creator; it abides in God and God is everywhere within it.

Celtic society was heroic and often warlike. It had its bondsmen and bondswomen, but there seems to have been none of the fear of Woman, manifested in the subjugation of women, such as we have known it in other Western societies. Nor is there any trace of that obsessional – and quite pathological – equation of sex with sin which has disfigured Western Christian spirituality for so long. Warrior Queens abounded, both in myth and in history; as both Maeve and Boudicca bear witness. The great Irish Hero Cúchulainn was taught his warrior's craft by a Scottish Warrior Queen and some of the most important spiritual initiatives of all were made by women, of whom Helen, the widow of Maxen Wledig (Magnus Maximus) was one and Bride of Kildare was another. Cattle rustling, rather than territorial conquest, was the main cause of internecine warfare, as the great Irish epic of the *Táin Bó Cúailnge* bears colourful witness.

# the coming of the faith

The Christian Faith came to the Celts in a variety of ways. It came to what is now England, and parts, at least, of Wales, with the Romans and, despite official disfavours and occasional persecutions, a considerable percentage of the population seems to have been at least nominally Christian by the time the Romans departed at the beginning of the fifth Century. They left, leaving the Celt urbanised and civilised in a very Roman sort of way. He began slowly to revert to his native ways but the almost immediate Anglo-Saxon invasions brought Teutonic paganism with them and forced the Celt and his Christian faith further and further West. They were eventually isolated in Wales, Cumbria and Cornwall, both from the rest of England and from each other. The later conversion of the Anglo-Saxons to the Faith is not our present concern, although the penultimate chapter will have something to say about it.

The Faith came to Scotland from two directions. First of all from Cumbria by means of Ninian's mission. Ninian (c.360-c.432) established himself initially at Whithorn in Galloway and then evangelised as far north as the Clyde and then some distance up the east coast. Much later, the Irishman, Colmcille, known in Scotland as Columba, (c.521-597) began a mission from a base on the isle of Iona, initially in support of the Irish who had established themselves in the Kingdom of *Dal Riada* in Argyll. Pagan Scotland was thereafter evangelised mostly from Ireland, but the Pictish Christian Church, founded by Ninian, existed in the east and centre of Scotland for four hundred years before the two somewhat different streams came finally together in the Ninth Century.

Ireland was a place of considerable missionary activity before ever Patrick arrived to join an existing mission in the south-east of the country. Patrick, (c.390-461) a Romano-British Celt, probably from Cumbria, initially organised the Church in continental fashion, with dioceses based on the courts of kings and tribal chiefs, many of whose sons became his clergy. Patrick knew his Ireland

and knew how to present the faith as the fulfilment of the best of the pagan hopes and dreams – the truth they were stumbling towards in their darkness. Ireland was substantially evangelised – though not completely converted – in his lifetime. But the urban style was foreign to Irish society, and Church organisation was quickly modified to a tribally-based monasticism, with the Abbot as superior and a Bishop (if he was not the Abbot himself) found from among his monks.

Cornwall, like Ireland, virtually untouched by the Romans and separated by distance from their urban centres, received the Faith principally through missions from Wales and from Ireland. There is a multitude of Cornish Saints, whose names are preserved in church dedications and of whom little or nothing is known, save for a mass of often confusing legend.

Northumbria, having had whatever Romano-British Christianity it may once have had blotted out by the Anglo-Saxons, returned to the Faith, first of all by the brief efforts of Paulinus, and then by the Irish mission of Aidan and others from Iona. The Synod of Whitby, in the year 664, set the Northumbrian Church firmly in line with the Continent and with Rome, and the Iona mission departed, but Northumbria showed the continuing influence of Celtic spirituality long after the Irish monks on Lindisfarne returned to Ireland.

# The Character of Celtic Spirituality

It will be clear from the few dates mentioned above that we are dealing with persons and events as much as four hundred years – perhaps longer – before a Latin monk, who is known to us as Saint Augustine of Canterbury, set foot on the coast of Kent in the year 597. Augustine's brief, apart from evangelising the Anglo-Saxons, was to bring the Roman-British Christian Church in Wales and the whole Western half of England into line with Rome. Though successful in his first task, it has to be said that he failed substantially in the second due, for the most part, to insensitivity and – let it be admitted – to sheer arrogance!

This fact of history may serve to encourage the idea, in the contemporary Western mind, that something called 'Celtic Christianity' once existed and is there to be rediscovered, to liberate us from the tiredness of everlastingly competing, and ever-increasingly expensive, ecclesiastical institutions. There is a 'back to nature' yearning, in a spiritual sense, which has manifested in forays into oriental religion, to the fringes of the occult and into do-it-yourself spirituality of every kind. Has this idea of an original 'Celtic Christianity' any basis in reality, or is it just another fantasy of tired minds? Is there indeed a forgotten Faith of the Christian West?

The answer is both 'yes' and 'no.'

It must be said at once that there is no such thing as 'Celtic Christianity' as something other than the Christian Faith as it is properly handed down to us. What there is, however, is a *Celtic Spirituality* which is undoubtedly closer to the primitive origins of the Faith than much of our contemporary forms in that it is essentially joyful and holistic and makes no unreal distinction between 'religion' and 'life.'

The first sense in which Celtic Spirituality is holistic is that it holds together, without fear, the two basic human faculties of reason and intuition. There is no 'airy-fairy' mysticism (true mysticism is anything but that!) and there is no spirit-numbing rationalism either. The Celtic Saints were intuitives whose feet were very firmly planted on the ground. It is their equilibrium as human beings which is much of their appeal, and in this, as in the holiness their lives display, they are Christlike.

The second sense in which Celtic Spirituality is holistic is that it knows no false distinctions between Earth and Heaven, between the farmer, his cow, the Saints, the Angels and the Lord Himself. There is no false dichotomy between 'sacred' and 'secular' because the whole of life, the whole of creation, is sacred. Celtic Spirituality is an uncluttered way of looking at things, it is a life lived with the mind in the heart, it is in fact the authentic Christian Faith to which all believers are called because it is quintessentially Christian.

Celtic Spirituality has nothing whatsoever to do with trying to be self-consciously 'Celtic,' or with founding communities of this and societies of that, or wearing funny clothes – or trying to be anything that one is not. It is to do with finding who one truly is, underneath all the present clutter of church institutions and world, *and being it by the grace of God.*

# Going places

We began this introductory chapter by remembering that there are times in all our lives when we discover that we are in 'a thin place,' a place that causes all the noise within us to be still and enables us, all unexpectedly, to "hear the sound that silence makes." Something has been said to the very depths of us; we don't know what it is that our spirit has heard but we "walk more slowly home" as the result of the hearing of it.

Many folk like visiting ancient holy places, places "where prayer has been valid" almost in the hope, or expectation, of experiencing whatever it is that they hope to find there! This is one of the spurs to pilgrimage, and pilgrimage is itself a prayer, for prayer is *something done* much more than it is something said.

This book will therefore indicate, in the course of its text, some of the places associated with the personalities with whom we shall become acquainted. Some are famous, many are not, but they are all places where the consecrated life has, as it were, soaked into the very ground. The very association of place with person is sufficient, however, for a truly 'thin place' can as easily challenge the unrealities within the visitor as it can sometimes speak comfortably to our souls. It is, in any event, a hazardous undertaking for anyone to go to a holy place simply looking for a 'psychic buzz'! As T.S.Eliot reminds us:

> ... human kind
> Cannot bear very much reality.
> (T.S.Eliot, *Burnt Norton*)

Pilgrimage is something done on a very different level than a day trip, but by the Grace of God the levels within us may change in the doing of it. But the reader must not expect to find easy and comfortable folk among the Celtic Saints. They are rugged and uncompromising men and women and they challenge us too deeply for any easy comfort. When we visit them, in the places that their consecration has consecrated, we do well to remember some other words of T.S.Eliot:

> You are not here to verify,
> Instruct yourself, or inform curiosity
> Or carry report. You are here to kneel
> Where prayer has been valid. And prayer is more
> Than an order of words, the conscious occupation
> Of the praying mind, or the sound of the voice praying.
> And what the dead had no speech for, when living,
> They can tell you, being dead: the communication
> Of the dead is tongued with fire beyond the language
> of the living.
> (T.S.Eliot, *Little Gidding*)

*chapter two*

# Obscure Beginnings

HERE CAN BE little doubt that the Christian Faith came to Britain with the Romans, almost certainly with individual believers in the army and in the civil administration. The main concern of this book will be with a period from about the middle of the Fourth Century to about the middle of the Eighth, but the foundations were laid some time after, and possibly quite soon after, the conquest of Britain by Claudius Caesar between the years 43 and 47.

The Celtic Britons, like their near relatives in Gaul, quickly adapted to the Roman administration and civilisation. An urban culture soon appeared with the development of towns and cities and the Christian Church was, in its earliest days, an essentially urban phenomenon following the Mediterranean pattern; the evangelisation of the rural population – the *pagani* – required new and quite different initiatives, as we shall see on a later page.

Individual Christians would meet fellow believers and they would make converts among their friends, acquaintances and neighbours. Thus the Church slowly put down roots, usually being tolerated but, from time to time, suffering ferocious, but generally short-lived persecutions. It is important to remember, however, that it was, initially at least, a Church without either a formal Creed or a New Testament as we know it. The canon of New Testament Scripture was not generally agreed until the early Fourth Century, nor were doctrines defined in formal creeds. There was no printing and therefore texts of any kind were probably a rarity for many years; everything had to be copied by hand. The Faith was therefore at its most primitive and found its main expression liturgically, in its Christ-given Sacraments of Baptism and the Eucharist. *The Apologies* of the Roman martyr Justin (d. 65 ) gives us something of its likely flavour.

The two historians, Gildas, a Briton (d. 570) and Bede, an Anglo-Saxon (d. 735), are our main sources of information, but they have their limitations. Gildas is unreliable about dates and is a highly subjective historian; Bede manifests a decided prejudice against the Romano-British – that is to say the Celtic – Church and against Celts in general. His dates have also to be treated with some caution although he is probably a good deal more reliable than Gildas. Bede tells us of a local British King, one Lucius, writing to Pope Eleutherius, in the middle of the Second Century, asking to be made a Christian. "The request was quickly granted and the Britons held the Faith which they received in all its purity until the time of the emperor Diocletian." The Christian Faith had become a *religio licita* (an officially permitted religion) in the year 260, but this did not prevent occasional persecutions from taking place, the most severe being that ordered by the Diocletian whom Bede mentions, in 303.

It would be most unwise, however, to assume that all, or even most, of the Romano-British population was Christian by the beginning of the Fourth Century but it seems certain that the Church was well and fairly peaceably established by then, with Diocesan Bishops in at least some of the main centres, and Metropolitans (we would now call them Archbishops) in the most important of them. Certain it is that at least three British Bishops, the Bishops of London, Lincoln and York, attended a council at Arles, in what is now France, in 314, and others the council at Ariminum in 359.

The Roman Commander-in-Chief in York, Constantius Chlorus, became Emperor in 292. His wife, Helen, had long been a Christian believer, though unbaptised until 312. Their son, Constantine, also an unbaptised believer, succeeded in 306 and, in 313, the year after his mother's baptism, the Christian Faith was granted official Imperial favour. It was now possible, among other things, for British Christians to build church buildings in which to celebrate their liturgy. Constantine himself was baptised on his death-bed, a not uncommon procedure at that time.

# "the seed of the church"

It has often been said that "the blood of the martyrs is the seed of the Church." Albanus (commonly known as St Alban) is the first Christian martyr in Britain whose name is known. His exact position in society is uncertain; he may have been a soldier or a member of the civil administration. There is no certainty that he was a Celt for the Roman army tended to use troops from other parts of the Empire for garrison purposes; locally recruited soldiers would normally be posted outside Britain. Whoever he was, he gave shelter to a Christian priest during a time of persecution. The holiness of the priest touched him, he took instruction and became a Christian himself and when his house was searched for the priest, who was known to be still at large, he wrapped himself in the priest's cloak and allowed himself to be arrested instead.

*The Acts of Alban*, quoted by Bede, gives a highly coloured account of his martyrdom. He was beheaded in the Roman city of Verulamium, but exactly when is uncertain; Bede gives the Diocletian persecution and 305 as the year of his death. But recent scholarship prefers the persecution under Decius of c.254, or even that under Septimus Severus in c.209. This latter is more consistent with his having been the first Christian martyr in Britain. Certain it is that the first mention of St Alban, the only Saint with a continuous cult from Roman times, is found in *The Life of Germanus of Auxerre* by Constantius of Lyons. This records a visit to St Alban's tomb at Verulamium by the Bishops Germanus and Lupus in 429. They removed some dust from it and gave relics of apostles and martyrs in return. The present-day name of Verulamium is St Albans.

Bede makes mention of two other Christians who were martyred in the same persecution, in *The City of Legions* (Caerleon-on-Usk). Their names were Aaron and Julius and "many others of both sexes throughout the land." But the dates, and indeed the specific persecutions during which they suffered, must be regarded as uncertain.

# Che Chronological Dilemma

The difficulty of finding an exact date for the first Christian martyrdom in Britain might seem to be surprising but there is a general uncertainty about the dating of individuals and events for perhaps the first five hundred years of the Common Era. It will be well worth our while to discover why this should be the case.

It was a Scythian monk, living in a Roman monastery in the early Sixth Century who invented the system of dating with which we are now familiar. Dionysius Exiguus (Dionysius the Obscure – his own, endearing and self-given description) was called upon to calculate a new cycle for the dating of Easter. He decided to abandon the then current Roman system of dating from the accession of the Emperor Diocletian in 284, and starting from the date of the foundation of the City of Rome, calculated – wrongly – that our Lord was born 753 years after that event.

He was between four and seven years late in that Herod the Great died in 4 BC and the Gospels make it quite clear that our Lord was born prior to that. Nevertheless, our Common Era, the Years of Grace, have been reckoned according to Dionysius' calculations since their adoption in Rome in 525. It was almost a century and a half later, at the Synod of Whitby in 664, that the Dionysian system was adopted in England. Every date prior to that has had to be recalculated at least once.

There was, however, another Roman system of calculating dates by the dates in office of the two Consuls. Another cleric, Victorius of Aquitaine, had already calculated an Easter Cycle, based on the 'two Consuls' system of dating. He started from the Passion and Resurrection and not from our Lord's birth, and arrived at the year 28 (Common Era) as the year of the Resurrection. Again, he was almost certainly wrong by a year or two. Current scholarship prefers the years 29, 30 or 33 as the date of the Resurrection.

The systems of Dionysius and Victorius were reconciled, but the fact that each was dating from the opposite end of our Lord's earthly life seems sometimes to have been forgotten. A possible error of some

28 years must therefore be accepted in cases where the date can not be cross-referenced from other sources. A further complication arises when it is remembered that until the introduction of the Gregorian calendar in the Sixteenth Century, New Year's Day was widely celebrated on Lady Day, 25th March. Another possible error of one year in any date must therefore be admitted.

The chronological dilemma is exemplified by the dates generally attributed to a man whose influence upon Celtic Christians in later generations than his own was to be profound. Anthony of Egypt is generally accepted to have died in 356, but the date of his birth is given as 251. This makes an exceedingly ascetic hermit one hundred and five years of age at his death. It is possible, but we are entitled to wonder if the 28-year possibility of error may have crept into the calculation of his birth-date.

Birth dates are, in any event, fraught with difficulties. Ages at death are often guesswork and birth dates are, equally often, calculations based upon guesswork. A man or a woman whose life has been memorable enough to be remembered as a Saint of God, attains to that status at the end of earthly life, not at its beginning. Heroic sanctity is sometimes only recognised for what it is some time after death; dates of birth must always be regarded as approximate at best.

# Attacks on the Integrity of the Faith

Threats, far more subtle to the integrity of the Roman-British Church than any of the periodic persecutions, came not from without, but from within. The early centuries of the Faith were troubled by one heresy after another until the Councils of the Church were compelled to define Christian doctrines in formulae which clearly and unambiguously established an orthodoxy. A heresy is an unbalanced or perverted statement of the Faith which, if left unchallenged, will pervert the revealed truth and lead believers badly astray. For the most part, the main heresies were attempts by intellectuals to reduce the Mystery to manageable proportions; to make the Incomprehensible comprehensible on their own terms. Bede tells of two such heresies which troubled the Romano-British Church for a time; one of them imported from the Mediterranean, the other very decidedly home-grown.

The Arian heresy, named after Arius, an Alexandrian priest who originated it, first made its appearance at about the time of Constantine's accession to the Imperial throne and, although condemned first by the Council of Nicea in 325, and then by the Council of Constantinople in 381, continued to trouble the Church (mainly in the Mediterranean area) for almost a century. It was a denial of the Divinity of Christ, an attempt to reduce the Incarnation to something that could be grasped by the intellect.

In brief, God was held to have created a Super-Creature through whom Creation was created. It was this Super-Creature (the *Demiurge*) who was born of the Virgin Mary and was made man. Superficially plausible, it reduced the Faith to the status of a mystery religion and effectively denied it altogether. It was the pressure of superficial intellectualisms, on every side, that compelled the Church to define her understandings both of the Holy Trinity and of the Incarnation, both Mysteries essentially being beyond all definition and entirely beyond the grasp of human intellect. The Creeds are therefore best understood as poetry as they reach faithfully, as only poetry can, beyond the possibilities of ordinary human articulation.

The Arian heresy is briefly mentioned by Bede. It had become a tool in Mediterranean power-politics but it seems not to have made much impact in Britain. The Pelagian heresy, however, the brain-child of a British monk in Rome, caused much more disturbance and was the occasion of intervention, twice, by Bishops from Gaul.

Pelagius came to Rome in the time of Pope Anastasius (399-401) where he soon acquired a considerable reputation for devotion and learning. Together with a close colleague and fellow-Briton, Celestius, he was aghast at the moral decadence of the whole of Roman society and the two of them, in their teaching, began to stress the responsibility of individuals for their own actions. Their doctrine of total freewill, and the responsibility for its exercise, seemed, however, to leave no room for the activity of Divine Grace. Pelagius reacted strongly against a quotation from his contemporary, Augustine of Hippo, who prayed to God, in relation to the gift of continence:

"Grant what thou commandest and command what thou wilt." This seemed to him to be a negation of the whole moral law, a positive abdication of personal responsibility. He was thus drawn into conflict with the mighty Augustine – of whom we shall hear more in a later chapter – and it is probable that, in the heat of controversy, both Pelagius and Celestius were provoked into extreme positions.

Celestius went so far as to deny that baptism is for the remission of sins and that there was indeed any such thing as original sin. Augustine was joined by Jerome in his attack on Pelagius and his apparent insistence than the individual could work out his own salvation without any help from the Divine Grace. At a series of Councils both Pelagius and Celestius were excommunicated and their teachings condemned. It was after the brief Pelagian furore in the Mediterranean was over that certain of their followers came to Britain and disturbed numbers of the Faithful with their superficially plausible but ultimately unfaithful and destructive teachings.

The British Bishops felt inadequate to the task of refuting this heresy and sought help from Gaul. Two Bishops, Germanus of Auxerre and Lupus of Troyes, visited Britain in 429 and effectively silenced the Pelagians at a conference at Verulamium. Germanus returned in 447 when the heresy resurfaced and, during his visit, became involved in a battle in which the Britons repulsed an incursion by a combination of Picts and Saxons. Both Germanus and Lupus are to be found in the Church's calendar of Saints.

# Two Seminal Influences

On the face of things it would seem strange that two seminal influences upon the Church in Britain, particularly after the end of the Roman period, should be an Egyptian hermit who seldom left the desert, and a Hungarian conscientious objector from the Roman army.

The establishment of the Christian Faith as the official religion of the Roman Empire in 313 opened the doors of the Church to politics and secularism. Before long the Imperial courts, both in the East and in the West, exercised enormous influence over the Church's life, not all of it benign. The Arian heresy was the first serious instance of rival Imperial factions cynically using a Christian doctrinal controversy for political ends.

In reaction to all this, and in reaction to the corruption and depravity of urban life in general, increasing numbers of Christians, both men and women, began to live the life of a hermit, usually in desert places. Anthony of Egypt was the one who brought order and recognition to the eremitical life and he provided a powerful inspiration to later generations; his influence was felt in Ireland and also in Wales where Dewi (known to us as St David), who died two hundred and fifty years after Anthony, was deeply inspired by his example.

It was a younger contemporary of Anthony, however, who was to have a fundamental influence upon the Church in England, Wales and Scotland. Martin was a Hungarian, a soldier and the son of an army officer. The date of his birth, variously given as 316 or 335, illustrates nicely the chronological dilemma to which we have referred. The date of his death is more reliably known as 397. Martin left the army, as a matter of conscience, after becoming a Christian believer. He became a pupil of Hilary, Bishop of Poitiers and, in 360, he chose the life of a hermit. So many others were attracted to his cell that, almost by inadvertence, he found himself the abbot of the first Christian monastery in Gaul.

After his consecration as Bishop of Tours, in 372, he continued living the monastic life but, in the context of his new responsibilities, he came to realise the potential of the monastic brotherhood as a tool for the evangelisation of the country folk who were largely untouched by the Gospel. These are the *pagani* from whom the word 'pagan' derives. It was the vision of Martin's monastic brotherhood, not as something in its own right, but as a vehicle of evangelism, that was to inspire a succession of Britons, returning home from the continental wanderings that seem to have been a feature of the *pax romana*.

Perhaps the most important of the many callers upon Martin and his community was the widow of Magnus Clemens Maximus, emperor in Britain, Gaul and Spain. The Western Imperial power was divided and, when an opportunity offered to seize the Imperial

Throne in Rome, Magnus took the bulk of his forces out of Britain, subcontracting the defence of the island to some trusted Celtic tribes during his absence. His wife, sometimes referred to as Helen of Caernarfon, accompanied him on his expedition, staying for some time at Trier. Magnus was defeated and killed and the newly widowed Helen, a Briton and a Christian believer, called upon Martin of Tours on her way home to Wales. She was fired with Martin's vision of a monastic brotherhood as a vehicle of rural evangelism and, beyond doubt, its manifestation in Wales within a generation or two owed a great deal to her influence.

There are a number of traditions concerning Helen. Her birthplace is claimed to have been Segontium (Caernarfon) and the road between Caernarfon and Carmarthen is known as Helen's Causeway (*Sarn Elen*). A romantic tale tells of how the emperor, Macsen Wledig (Magnus Maximus) fell in love with a beautiful woman who appeared to him in a dream. She was discovered in Segontium and her name was Elen Luyddog. The name Elen belongs to Welsh mythology and it is likely that Magnus' widow became identified with one of the three sisters of the mythical Arianrhod, who lived with her in her castle in the depths of the sea. These three, Gwennan, Maelan and Elen, appear to be Celtic goddesses associated with the dawn.

Our Helen was probably neither 'of Caernarfon' nor a goddess, but simply the Christian widow of an unsuccessful claimant to the Imperial Throne. She is most reliably believed to have been the daughter of the local British King of Erging, whose territory was centred upon Ariconium (Weston-under-Penyard) near Ross on Wye. This good Monmouthshire lass has given her name to a number of Welsh churches, and also to Llanelen in West Gower. Both 22 May and 25th August are given as her feast day.

# The Coming of the Darkness

So far we have covered the period of the Roman occupation of Britain which ended at the beginning of the Fifth Century. It will be worth our while to examine the circumstances which have caused practically the whole of that century to become obscured and, as a consequence, have caused the remarkable men and women we refer to as the Celtic Saints to shine with such brilliance in the two centuries that followed.

The Roman occupation was fatally flawed in that it was incomplete. The attempt to extend the Empire into Scotland was an expensive failure. The Antonine Wall, the northerly fixed line of defence, was soon abandoned and Hadrian's Wall was strengthened to become, half 'Maginot Line,' half customs post, holding at arm's length the barbarians of the North and regulating both trade and the passage of individuals. Ireland seems to have been untouched by Imperial Rome.

Fixed fortifications tend to induce a defensive cast of mind and the initiative is handed to potential enemies. As the Fourth Century unfolded these made their presence felt ever more powerfully. Beyond the Wall, up to the estuaries of the Forth and Clyde, the native Celtic people were essentially the same as those in Southern Cumbria (Brigantia) and spoke a Celtic language from which the later Welsh and Cornish developed. South of the Wall there is reason to believe that a substantial part of the population was Christian by this time. North of the Wall, although there may have been small pockets of Christian believers, for the most part they worshipped the old gods.

North of the Forth and Clyde were the Picts, divided, as it would appear, into Southern and Northern kingdoms. These formidable folk, who left no written records and whose language has vanished, seem to have been of at least part-Celtic stock and to have spoken a mixture of Brythonic (i.e. Welsh and Cornish) Celtic and, perhaps, an older, Indo-European language. But all this is largely a matter of speculation for no written records of them survive.

The Irish (whom Bede calls the Scots) spoke a different, possibly older, Celtic language and had already begun their incursions into the Western Highlands. They were frequent raiders all along the west coast of Britain. There were invasions of both North and South Wales and there were Welsh and Pictish raids into Northern Ireland. For several centuries in these turbulent times the Irish-speaking Welshman and the Welsh (or Pictish) speaking Irishman were both to be encountered as we shall see in the pages that follow.

In the year 360, the probable year of the birth of Ninian, of whom we shall have much to say in a following chapter, there seems to have been a concerted assault upon Northern England by the Southern Picts and Scotti from Ireland. Seven years later, a more serious assault was made by the same forces, but this time they were joined by a new and menacing force, the Teutonic Angles from North Germany and Southern Scandinavia. The Wall was breached and Southern Cumbria overrun.

The situation was serious indeed in that there is evidence both of treachery among the frontier scouts and also a breakdown of discipline in the regular forces. Deserters and barbarians alike plundered as far south as London. The two highest ranking military officers came to grief; the Duke of the Britons, who commanded the frontier garrison, was captured and the Count of the Saxon Shore, in charge of the coastal defences against pirates, was killed. Such was the pressure on other parts of the Empire at that time that had the barbarians been intent on actual conquest rather than on looting, Britain would very probably have been lost to the Roman Empire altogether.

The situation was restored by Count Theodosius in 369. He granted an amnesty to the disaffected soldiery and won their allegiance by a mixture of common sense and firmness. The land was reconquered, the Wall repaired, the damaged forts rebuilt and the unreliable frontier scouts were disbanded. At the same time, a pro-Roman tribe North of the Wall, the Votadini, were brought into treaty alliance with Rome and charged with the defence, North of the Wall, against the still hostile Picts.

It may have been at about this time (or possibly later as a fruit of this treaty relationship) that the war-lord Cunedda was induced to migrate, with eight sons and one grandson, from Manau Guotidin (Votadini land near Stirling) to North-West Wales in order to drive out the invading Irish. It is doubtful if the Cambrian Mountains and their tribes had ever been under effective Roman control.

The date of Cunedda's hiring as a mercenary or *dux bellorum*, with an associated gift of territory, is uncertain. It is probable that it took place a generation later than Theodosius and was incidental to the attempt to seize the Imperial Throne by Magnus Maximus between 383 and 388. There is a tradition, and indeed a distinct likelihood, that the shadowy figure of Vortigern, usually blamed for introducing Anglo-Saxon mercenaries to defend Britain against the Anglo-Saxons, was a son-in-law of Magnus and Helen. Vortigern is a title (The High Chief) and not a personal name, however, and anything said about him has to be qualified in view of the great confusion surrounding the whole period between the end of the Fourth and the beginning of the Sixth Centuries.

Magnus Maximus may fairly be blamed for finally sacrificing Romano-British security and civilisation on the altar of his own ambition. A quarter of a century after his death the Romans abandoned Britain to its own devices altogether. Helen, his wife and widow, represents the one redeeming feature of that whole unhappy episode.

*chapter three*

# Ninian: A Cumbrian in Scotland

*When the true shepherd speaks, and man hears him,*
*the heart burns within,*
*the flesh trembles,*
*the mind lights like a candle*
*the conscience ferments like wine in a crock,*
*and the will bows to the truth,*
*and that small, powerful heavenly voice*
*raises up the dead from his own grave to live,*
*to don the crown,*
*and wonderfully changes the whole of life*
*to live like the Lamb of God.*

Morgan Llwyd[1]

T THE MIDDLE of the turbulent last century of Roman-occupied Britain, there was born to Cumbrian Christian parents a son whom we know by the name of Ninian. There is a tradition that he was the son of the chief of a Cumbrian tribe, the Novantes, and that he was born in or near Whithorn, where he was later to found his community.

At that time, Cumbria extended from just north of the river Clyde to the river Derwent in Lakeland, and in the east it included the Lothians, Berwickshire and Northumberland. Cumbria was thus only partially Roman, but, south of Hadrian's wall, its southern half was the well administered Roman province of Brigantia. Roman influence extended north of the wall, however, and there was a Roman fort at Locopibium, close to the present Whithorn in Galloway.

Ninian's family was, like all other Cumbrian Christians, in the somewhat remote pastoral care of the already important bishops of York. His biographer, Aelred of Rievaulx, tells us that "He was sparing in food, reticent in speech, assiduous in study, agreeable in manners." The young Ninian soon experienced a sense of vocation. As Aelred describes it: "What," said he, "shall I do? I have sought in my own land Him whom my soul loves. I sought Him, but I have not found Him. I will arise now, and I compass sea and land. I will seek the truth which my soul loves." [2]

# Jouaneys and Missions

As soon as he reached manhood, therefore, in his late teens, Ninian travelled to Rome where he was received by the Pope, Damasus I, and studied the Faith under such formidable teachers as Jerome, the aged Pope's secretary. Jerome was a scholar of quite outstanding brilliance with a personality better suited to the making of enemies than friends. He was, at that very time, working on his monumental translation of the Hebrew Bible and the New Testament into Latin. Jerome's translation was to become known as the *Vulgate* and, until the Reformation, it was to be the only authorised version of Holy Scripture for Western Christians. It was an exceedingly fortunate time for the young Ninian to be in Rome.

Damasus' successor, Siricius, sent Ninian back to own people and consecrated this still very young man Bishop, probably in the year 394. On his way back to Britain, Ninian visited Martin of Tours, at what is now Marmoutier, but which name is derived from the Celtic word, *muinntir*, meaning 'family.' The 'family' was, of course, the monastic family which Martin had gathered about himself; it was at once an evangelistic powerhouse, a theological college, Martin's Diocesan headquarters and the mutual support-group for the activities of all its members.

Ninian realised at once that Martin, this holy, innovative genius, already deeply suspected by more conventionally-minded Church leaders, was the man from whom he would learn how to set about his chosen work. The tasks for which he had been consecrated Bishop were to evangelise his fellow-Cumbrian Celts, who dwelt north of Hadrian's Wall, and then to take the Gospel to the Pictish people who were, as yet, untouched by it. Ninian resolved to emulate Martin. He would gather about himself a *muinntir*, a family of brethren, consecrated to Mission, and he would establish a community on the lines of that at Tours. This was a proven instrument for the effective evangelisation of country districts. It related to the structure of Celtic society, it spoke to its needs. In short, it worked!

The influence of Martin is found in the name given to the community Ninian founded at Whithorn in, or after, the year 397. Martin's original cell on Bishop Hilary's farm at Poitiers had been known as the 'White Hut.' An early Irish name for Ninian's foundation, where the community dwelt, was *Taigh Martain*, 'House of Martin.' It was also known, in Latin, as *Candida Casa*, or 'The White House,' and it is by this name that it has been remembered, by Christians, for sixteen hundred years. Latin writers also referred to it as *Magnum Monasterium*, a direct translation of *Mormuinntir*, 'the big family.'

Ninian reproduced Martin of Tours' arrangements in detail. Martin had his own cave, or retreat, in the sandstone rocks at Marmoutier and so Ninian found himself a cave in the rocks on the shore at Glasserton, not far from Candida Casa.

Having established his community and thoroughly prepared both himself and them, Ninian began the serious work of evangelising Scotland in about the year 400. He was not only active in Scotland, however, for there are strong Irish traditions of his work among the Brythonic Celtic speakers of Ulster. The fruits of this work were going to be of incalculable benefit to Ninian's successors in later generations. Ninian followed the example of Martin of Tours and established the beginnings of a parochial system whereby there is a priest and a congregation of the Faithful responsible for the evangelisation and the pastoral care of a particular area. Aelred of Rievaulx, who wrote (or rather edited and rewrote) Ninian's *Life* in the Twelfth Century, tells us that he began to ordain priests, consecrate bishops, distribute the other dignities of the ecclesiastical ranks and, having "confirmed in faith and good works the sons whom he had begotten in Christ, and having set in honour all things that referred to the honour of God and the welfare of souls, he bade the brethren farewell and returned to his own church" (Candida Casa).

Ninian had left Rome at a time of comparative theological peace. The most dangerous of the great heresies, Arianism, which effectively denied the Divinity of Christ, was condemned at the great Council of Nicea, thirty years before he was born. By this time the doctrinal position of the Christian Church was more or less defined and the process of definition was to be completed at the Council of Chalcedon, during his lifetime. Ninian and his mission were thus untroubled by the doctrinal upheavals of the Fourth and early Fifth Centuries.

# Associates and Contemporaries

A mighty champion of Christian orthodoxy and an exact contemporary of Ninian was Augustine of Hippo. He was also – alas! – to become the unwitting agent of a profound disturbance of the Christian corporate peace of mind for, when he was baptised in 386, eight years before Ninian left Rome, he brought with him, unconsciously, a profound and unresolved sexual guilt, and as a consequence of this, Augustine's attitude to women owed a great deal more to his own deeply tangled psychology than to any kind of Christian theology.

Augustine is a seminal influence in Western theology, though less revered in the Christian East. He is undoubtedly a towering figure for whom, for the most part, we have reason to be deeply grateful. But he was flawed, and the unbalanced side of his personality and teaching has had an unfortunate effect upon the Western Christian approach both to sexuality and – far worse – to women. Tragically, the Reformation, instead of correcting this distortion, proceeded rather to emphasise it. In particular the Calvinistic doctrine of 'total depravity' carries Augustine's doctrine of Original Sin a good deal further, and paints it even blacker, than ever Augustine himself did.

We shall consider Augustine and his legacy at greater length in our final chapter but, in this connection it may be noted that even the waspish Jerome had women among his students. The names of three of them are known to us: Paula, Marcella and Eustochium. They were widows and, with others, were attempting to live a semi-monastic life in a city that lived by sensuality. Poor Jerome was to be the subject of scandalous gossip for his pains. Apparently, it was completely – even ridiculously – unjustified.

# miꞦacles and Legends

The primitive Faith holds nothing to be impossible. Stories of Ninian's healing miracles abound and whereas an earlier generation than our own indulged in scepticism and 'demythologising,' we are now readier than our immediate predecessors were to accept the realities of the Church's Ministry of Healing. Healing is, in fact, Love's response to human afflictions; it accompanies the preaching of the Gospel almost automatically, in some form or another. Ninian's own miracles – many revealing a supernatural intuition – all show, among other things, an immense compassion for sinners, a great gentleness, and an entirely delightful sense of humour.

A prophet is seldom respected in his own land, however, and Aelred tells us of a local petty king, one Tuduvallus "whom riches, power and honour had made proud, and in whom lasciviousness and worldly wealth had so bred haughtiness that he presumed himself to be all-powerful and believed that what anyone else could do was both possible and lawful to him also." (An ever-contemporary figure!) "He, despising the admonitions of the man of God, secretly deprecated his doctrine and manners, and openly opposed his sound teaching."

Tuduvallus became seriously ill, however. As Aelred puts it, God "struck him on the head with an unbearable disease." He became blind and "the poor man lay oppressed by pain, deprived of sight, darkened externally" but, in consequence "lightened internally." He came to repentance. Ninian, who had suffered a great deal from this man, treated him "with the greatest kindness and devotion ... touching the head of the sick man with healing hand, he signed the blind eyes with the sign of the saving life (the Cross). The pain fled, the blindness was driven away by the coming light, and so it came to pass that the disease of the body cured the disease of the soul, and the power of the man of God expelled the disease of the body." [3]

Parish clergy, then as now, are very vulnerable to false accusations and Aelred tells us of one young woman who allowed herself to be seduced by an importunate young man, and who became pregnant as a consequence. To escape punishment she claimed that she had been seduced by the parish priest!

> "The good were scandalized, the wicked elated, the common people laughed, and the sacred order was scoffed at; the presbyter, whose fame was injured, was saddened. But the innocence of the priest by the revelation of the Spirit was not hidden from the bishop beloved by God. He bore, however, with impatience the scandal to the Church and the injury to holy religion."

On Ninian's next visit to the congregation, the girl thrust her baby up into the priest's face and accused him, in the presence of everyone, of being the child's father. Ninian then addressed the child and commanded it, in the name of God, to identify its real father. This the child proceeded to do, pointing to the young man and – according to legend – speaking with a grown man's voice, acknowledged him as its father. [4]

One of his miracles – a curiously domestic miracle – reveals in Ninian both an impish sense of fun as well as a Christ-like authority over nature. It speaks both of his personality and of his compassion. In the refectory one day, noticing a dearth of vegetables on the table, he called for the gardener of the community and gave him a gentle rebuke for not having grown any leeks. The poor man complained that he had only planted them the day before. "Go and see what you can find," said Ninian. The gardener then discovered a garden full of fully-grown leeks!

"He was astonished and, as if in a trance, thought that he saw a vision. Finally, returning to himself, and calling to mind the power of the holy man ... he ... placed (them) on the table before the bishop." [5]

# ⚜ The Spirituality of Ninian

Ninian, and the Roman-British Church which had nurtured him, was quite untouched by the world-rejecting tendencies of contemporary Mediterranean Christianity, and Celtic spirituality as a whole shows no signs of having been tarred by the Augustinian brush. That two British Christians of the next generation, Pelagius and Celestius, were so aghast at the moral decadence of the City of Rome as to begin a crusade against it, albeit hasty and ill thought out, suggests that a healthier and more normal life was being lived back home in Britain. The healthier Celtic attitude to women prevailed and there are references to women coming to study the Faith at Whithorn, certainly in later years. It was the primitive and essentially uncomplicated Faith that crossed the water, both to and from Whithorn and, within little more than thirty years, it had spread to the Clyde, crossed the Forth, and had made its way up the eastern half of Scotland as far as the Isles of Orkney and of Shetland.

Ninian does not appear to have limited himself to the Scottish mainland, however. There is good cause to believe that he crossed the North Channel and began missionary work among the Brythonic-speaking Celts in the north-east of Ireland, conveniently known as the Irish Picts. Nearly opposite Candida Casa, in the shelter of what is now known as Strangford Loch, a *muinntir* was established at 'n-Aondruim (corrupted to Nendrum – the original Brythonic form of Ninian was Non, or Nen). The brethren of Aondruim were dependent on Candida Casa, ships from Whithorn were in the habit of calling there and Caolan, the second Ab (Abbot) of Aondruim sent Finnian, later the founder of Moville, to Candida Casa for the purpose of completing his education. The first Ab of Aondruim is said to have been Mochaoi, the son of Bronag, daughter of Maelchon, the man to whom Ninian's contemporary, Patrick, was a slave for six years.

Candida Casa had a far bigger share in the conversion of Ireland than is usually realised. Finbar, in the Sixth Century, established his own *muinntir* at Maghbile on his return from Whithorn, and Comgall the Great founded the most famous of all the *muinntirs* at Bangor. What we may describe as the spiritual cross-fertilisation between the various *muinntirs*, and also with the Welsh *Llans*, was probably perpetual and certainly mutually beneficial. The great Dewi (St David, patron Saint of Wales) may well have learned his monasticism in Ireland and there is more than a suggestion that he had also been a welcome visitor to the Candida Casa community of his own day.

# Tracing St Ninian on the Ground

Celtic foundations bear the name of their founder. It was many centuries before dedications of churches to particular canonised Saints in an official Church Calendar became a feature of Scottish Church life, and then they tended to be dedicated to non-Celtic Saints. It is thus easier than might be supposed to identify places and dates by their ancient names. First of all, however, we have to reconcile the map of Scotland as we know it with that of Ptolemy, which the untravelled Bede uses in all his references to the period. Ptolemy drew a map which showed Scotland at right-angles to England! Bede's references to South are therefore to what is actually the East and all his other compass points have to be adjusted accordingly. The scope of Ninian's mission was, first of all, to the north to what is now Glasgow, then to the east and then up the east coast as far as Orkney and Shetland. We may uncover his activities by the place names which reveal him as founder.

From Whithorn and the site of Candida Casa we travel north to St Ninian's Colmonell in Ayrshire; thence to 'Kil Sanct Ninian' at Ardmillan, also in Ayrshire; from there to what is now St

Mungo's Cathedral in Glasgow, built on the site of one of Ninian's foundations.

From Glasgow we turn north-east and then east, to St Ninian's Church, Stirling; to Coupar in Angus where 'St Ninian's Lands' are to be found, and then to Arbirlot in Forfarshire where there is a St Ninian's Well. There is 'St Ninian's Inch' at Arbroath, in Forfarshire. This refers to a stretch of pasture land by the shore, close to St Ninian's Well at Seaton.

The geographical shape of Ninian's missionary activity is clear: from extreme south-west to the Highland Line, then to the east coast. Once at the east coast the direction is northwards.

At Dunottar Castle in Kincardineshire, an extension made in about 1380 uncovered the remains of St Ninian's church; *Annat* (Mother Church), Methlick, Aberdeenshire; St Ninian's, Pit Medan, Aberdeenshire (Medan was a near contemporary of Ninian and the prefix 'Pit' denotes a Pictish origin); St Ninian's, Fochabers, Morayshire; St Ninian's Diser (corruption of a word for a clerical retreat), believed to be at Dyke in Moray; *An Teampull* or *Teampull Rinian*, Loch Ness, Inverness-shire; Fearn, Edderton, Rosshire, the original site of the Celtic Abbey of Fearn.

We have gone a long way up the map, but there is further to go, first to St Ninian's, Navidale (Ni'andal) Sutherland; St Ninian's, Head of Wick, where the inlet is known as Papigoe, or the Cleric's inlet. Thence to the Orkneys to St Ninian's North Ronaldsay and on to the Shetlands where, on St Ninian's Isle, Dunrossness, a stone with Ogham characters reveals that the site was occupied by members of St Ninian's *muinntir*.

Bearing in mind that the dedication of church buildings and sites to patron saints was unknown among Celts until the Eighth Century, and among the Picts not at all, and that all personal names referred to the original founder, we have an astonishing witness, all over the Scottish landscape, to the faith and life's work of an astonishing person. To what extent the Picts were converted to the Faith we cannot know but the site-names indicate at least pockets of the Faithful among them.

Ninian was a son of the Roman-British Church of Britain, a North Cumbrian. We must now turn our attentions to another, a contemporary of Ninian and also a Cumbrian. His name is Patrick.

1 *Gweithiau Morgan Llwyd O Wynedd*, Thomas Ellis (Jarvis Foster, Bangor, 1899)
2 *Saint Ninian*, Aelred of Rievaulx, ed. Iain MacDonald (Floris, Edinburgh, 1993) pp.23-24)
3 ibid. pp.32-33
4 ibid. pp.34-37
5 ibid. pp.41-42

## chapter four

# Patrick: A Cumbrian in Ireland

*I arise today*
*through a mighty strength,*
*the invocation of the Trinity,*
*through belief in the Threeness,*
*through confession of the Oneness*
*of the Creator of Creation* [1]

**W**E KNOW remarkably little of this remarkable man other than from his own pen. His name was Magonus Sucatus Patricius and he was the son of a Romano-British official of some standing, the holder of an obligatory civil office, that of decurion. He may therefore have been a Roman citizen. Patrick tells us that his father, Calpurnius, was also in deacon's orders in the Church and that his father, Patrick's grandfather Potitus, was a Christian priest. The likely date of Patrick's birth was 389. He describes himself as having been ignorant of God in his early years but, shortly before the age of sixteen, he was taken prisoner by Irish pirates and sold into slavery in Ireland.

Many places on the west coast of Britain claim to be the birthplace of Patrick, from North Devon to Southern Scotland, but the probable location of Banna venta Bernia is close to the fort of Birdoswald on the Roman Wall. Bernia, which means a mountain pass, may refer to the nearby Greenhead Pass. If we make a guess that Potitus was fifty years of age when his grandson was born we have a picture of a fairly well established Christian presence, in the context of the religious peace that followed Constantine's accession to the Imperial throne.

Patrick's *Confession*, written in his old age, tells of his life as a shepherd in the West of Ireland, for six years. The experience of slavery woke up his dormant Faith and he tells us of a life given to prayer at every opportunity, day and night and in all weathers. "I felt no harm," he tells us, "and there was no sloth in me – as I now see, because the spirit within me was then fervent. And there one night I heard in my sleep a voice saying to me: 'it is well that you fast, soon you will go to your own country.' And again, after a short while, I heard a voice saying to me: 'See, your ship is ready.' And it was not near, but at a distance of perhaps two hundred miles, and I had never been there, nor did I know a living soul there; and then I took to flight, and I left the man with whom I had stayed for six years. And I went in the strength of God who directed my way to my good, and I feared nothing until I came to that ship." [2]

The ship seems to have been bound for Gaul and to have been carrying, amongst other things, Irish hounds. There were more adventures, more hardships and even captivities, but "after many years" Patrick came home to his own folk in Britain, where he devoutly wished to remain for the rest of his life.

It was not to be.

"And there I saw in the night the vision of a man, whose name was Victoricus, coming as it were from Ireland, with countless letters. And he gave me one of them, and I read the opening words of the letter, which were: 'The voice of the Irish.' And as I read the beginning of the letter I thought that at the same moment I heard their voice – they were those beside the Wood of Voclut, which is near the Western Sea – and thus did they cry out as with one mouth: 'We ask thee, boy, come and walk among us once more.'

And I was quite broken in heart, and could read no further, and so I woke up. Thanks be to God, after many years the Lord gave to them according to their cry." [3]

# Che Mission of palladius

We must leave Patrick for a while and go to Auxerre in Gaul where the redoubtable Germanus was bishop. Prosper of Aquitaine, in his *Chronicle,* mentions the name Palladius twice and it is probable that he is referring to the same person on both occasions. In 429, Palladius was sent to Rome, probably to obtain papal sanction for Germanus' intervention into the affairs of the British Church in the matter of the Pelagian heresy. Piecing together what evidence there is, it seems likely that Palladius accompanied the bishops Germanus and Lupus to Britain and returned to Rome to report on the outcome. He was a deacon, possibly of Auxerre, but there is also a suggestion that he was a deacon of Rome itself.

Prosper tells us that, in 431, the same Pope Celestine consecrated him bishop and sent him to Ireland, to the Irish believers in the south-east of Ireland. Palladius worked mainly in Wicklow where three churches are named as of his foundation, at Tigonry, Donard and Cilleen Cormac (near Dunlavin). But his was an episcopate of only two or three years. Some sources say that he died, others that, for whatever reason, he left Ireland and preached in Scotland for twenty-three years before dying at Forddun. There is evidence of a cult of Palladius in Aberdeen. He will therefore have come under the aegis of Candida Casa and even, possibly, of Ninian himself. But this is a matter of conjecture, we know nothing for certain.

Patrick, who by this time was in Holy Orders, possibly in Britain, possibly in Gaul, was sent to Ireland to assist Palladius. By the time he arrived, Palladius was no longer there and so he returned to Gaul and, in spite of some opposition, mainly from British clerics, was consecrated bishop and sent to replace Palladius in Ireland.

The opposition to Patrick's consecration centred upon two things: his education was rudimentary and his Latin was, to say the least, rough and ready. He describes himself as "a rustic." But there had also been a breach of confidence by a friend and fellow cleric to whom Patrick had made his confession before he was made deacon. There had been a moral lapse of some kind in his teenage years and this was advanced as evidence of his unsuitability for the episcopate. Patrick refers to this in his *Confession* and was evidently deeply hurt by it.

Patrick's own missionary activity was not based in Wicklow. He travelled north, and Armagh became the centre of his activities. Armagh is, in fact, the one site which can be associated with him with any certainty. To such an extent did Patrick become a legend in his own lifetime that namings and dedications of wells and of all manner of things are to be found all over the country. Even Croagh Patrick, Downpatrick and the St Patrick's Purgatory are not sites with which he can be identified with any real historical certainty.

# Che Style of patrick's mission

Patrick had a great advantage over certain other evangelists who had preceded him. He thoroughly understood Irish society and he knew where power and influence lay. He seems, therefore, to have concentrated upon the courts of kings and chiefs, and with notable success, despite many setbacks and not a little danger. He chose his clergy from the sons of the Irish nobility and, although not a monastic himself, he greatly encouraged any who felt a call to the monastic life, both men and women. He tells us:

> "Among others, a blessed Irishwoman of noble birth, beautiful, full-grown, whom I had baptized, came to us after some days for a particular reason: she told us that she had received a message from a messenger of God, and he admonished her to be a virgin of Christ and draw near to God. Thanks be to God, on the sixth day after this she most laudably and eagerly chose what all virgins of Christ do. Not that their fathers agree with them; no – they often suffer persecution and undeserved reproaches from their parents; and yet their number is ever increasing." [4]

In his *Confession*, Patrick is revealed as a passionate and totally dedicated man and also a very appealing personality. He is under no illusions about his indifferent education but is vividly clear about his vocation and its responsibilities; his *Letter to Coroticus*, however, shows a man of steel underneath the self-confessed "rustic".

Coroticus was almost certainly the Welsh prince Ceredig, founder of the principality of Ceredigion (Cardigan). The departure of the Romans at the very beginning of the Fifth Century had left a power vacuum which was filled by local princes, and Coroticus (Ceredig), himself a Christian believer, had become defender of Romano-British Christians against the very Irish raiders who had abducted Patrick in his youth.

Before long Coroticus had become strong enough to launch reprisal raids against Ireland and, on one of these raids, his men attacked a newly baptised Christian community, killed several and abducted the rest into slavery. A letter of protest from Patrick, asking for the release of captives, was scornfully dismissed and Patrick was provoked into sending a letter of furious denunciation to Coroticus, demanding retribution.

> "With my own hand I have written and composed these words, to be given, delivered, and sent to the soldiers of Coroticus. I do not say, to my fellow citizens, or to fellow citizens of the holy Romans, but to fellow citizens of the demons, because of their evil works ... Dripping with blood, they welter in the blood of innocent Christians whom I have begotten into the number for God and confirmed in Christ! ... I do not know what to lament more: those who have been slain, or those whom they have taken captive, or those whom the devil has snared." [5]

In the *Letter to Coroticus*, as in the *Confession*, Patrick's sense of rejection by his own Romano-British brethren surfaces, almost with bitterness, "... my own people do not know me, 'a prophet hath no honour in his own country.' ... I am hated. What shall I do, Lord? I am most despised." [6]

Emphasising, again and again, the monstrous sin that has been committed, contrasting the heavenly state of the slain with the retribution to come for Coroticus and his soldiery, Patrick ends his letter with a prayer for their repentance.

> "May God inspire them sometime to recover their senses for God, repenting, however late, their heinous deeds – murderers of the brethren of the Lord – and to set free the baptized women whom they took captive, in order that they may deserve to live to God, and be made

whole, here and in eternity! Be peace to the Father, and to the Son, and to the Holy Spirit. Amen." [7]

# A Remarkable Virgin of Christ

One of the virgins of Christ to whom Patrick refers in his Confession was Brigid, daughter of Dubthach, son of Demre, son of Bresal, of the sept of Echaid Find Fuathnairt. Dubthach is said to have bought a slave-girl by the name of Dallbronach and fathered a child on her. Dubthach's wife was consumed by jealousy and wanted the slave-girl out of the house, especially after two bishops from Scotland – so tradition has it – were guests of Dubthach and made certain prophesies concerning the still-unborn child. In the end, Dubthach sold his slave-girl to a poet who sold her on to a wizard, and the same tradition has it that she was eventually brought up in the household of a local king. This latter seems most unlikely.

All of this is probably a mixture of romantic storytelling and mythology, with a just-sufficient bare thread of fact underneath all the embroidery to present us with the real person at the end of it all. It would be very agreeable to think that the "blessed Irishwoman of noble birth, beautiful, full-grown, whom I had baptized," was the Brigid of history, but there is no evidence of this whatsoever. Nevertheless the historical Brigid, whatever her background, found a vocation to the monastic life and became a virgin of Christ.

*The Book of Lismore* gives an astonishing account of the occasion when Brigid, with seven others, took the veil. They were to be professed by a Bishop Mel in Telcha Mide. Brigid wished to be the last to be professed but she was called out to the front by the bishop, whereupon "it came to pass then, through the grace of the Holy Ghost, that the form of ordaining a bishop was read out over Brigid. Mac-caille said that a bishop's order should not be conferred on a woman. Bishop Mel said: 'No power have I in this matter. That dignity has been given by God unto Brigid, beyond every other woman.' Wherefore the men of Ireland from that time to this give episcopal honour to Brigid's successor." [8]

It is difficult to know what to make of this story. It would probably be as unwise to dismiss it out of hand as to build confident theories upon it.

Brigid was a much younger contemporary of Patrick and the two were apparently well acquainted, indeed he seems to have baptized her himself. Bishop Mel was one of the two which tradition had as "coming from Scotland" and, if he was an actual historical person, he might well have had connections with Candida Casa and its Ulster offshoots whom Patrick, in any event, cannot fail to have known and worked closely with. Certain it is that Brigid, like Patrick, became a legend in her own lifetime and has gathered to herself a wealth of legend, mythology and sheer fairy-story, all of which shows her in a most attractive light.

It is said that Brigid was one of eight to take the veil on that occasion, according to the eight beatitudes of the Gospel, and that the beatitude she chose for herself was The Merciful. There is, however, another attribute to the historical Brigid, for she very quickly became strongly identified with the pre-Christian Celtic goddess of the same name.

# Che UniveRsal feminine pRinciple

There is a fundamental feminine principle in creation, an archetypal energy of some kind, which finds universal expression as 'the goddess' under all manner of guises. Early Celtic and pre-Celtic religion, as far as we are able to discern it from the ancient mythologies, operated under a Sky-Father and Earth-Mother principle. There was a principle 'good god,' Dagda, and the consort, Dana, was essentially the Earth-Mother. Offspring of these two were the various gods and goddesses, often in groups of three, and one of the legendary offspring of Dagda was Brigid who, being an essentially benign and attractive personality, became identified with many of the functions of the Earth-Mother herself. There were no formal creeds in ancient religion and confusion of the functions of what, like all pagan gods and goddesses, were basic archetypal energies, was very common.

Celtic religion had no goddess of love, there was no Aphrodite to enliven the pantheon, but Brigid was a goddess of wisdom, which included esoteric knowledge of all kinds. She was regarded as the special patron of poets, smiths and healers. (Strictly, there are three Brigids; Brigid the goddess of poets, Brigid the smith and Brigid the healer.) Brigid is the true 'mother of memory,' who fosters the creative and magical arts. Brigid's feast of Imbolc (1st February) marks the coming of new life after the 'night' in which the year is born. She is 'the Fair Maid of Spring.'

Brigid – often called Bride – represents, in the Celtic pre-Christian tradition, the 'goddess of mercy,' the motherly Bodissatva Guanyin in the Buddhism of China and indeed Tara, the young woman manifestation of the same archetypal principle in Tibet. In the Celtic Christian tradition there is a twofold fulfilment to be found. The Blessed Virgin Mary, Mother of the Incarnate Lord, is the ultimate fulfilment of this entire universal feminine principle, indeed we might almost regard her as the historical incarnation of it. Upon Brigid, or Bride, however, the historical virgin of Christ, a woman revered for holiness and as the very embodiment of feminine compassion, has fallen the mantle of the much-loved pre-Christian goddess. It is not too much to say that the two are almost inextricably intertwined.

It is not only Brigid the virgin of Christ and Brigid the pagan goddess that are intertwined for, in the Celtic Christian tradition there is a profound mythology which links Mary and Brigid as close friends and companions, however impossible the actual chronology might be. Brigid was, in this tradition, the midwife at the birth of Jesus the Christ in Bethlehem. She it was, in this tradition, who searched with Mary for the twelve-year-old Jesus and found him in the Temple among the doctors of the law. Delightfully, Brigid is supposed to have used her psychic gift of 'skrying' in order to find out where the boy was! Such is her close, near-identification with Mary the Mother of God, that St Brigid is often referred to, as in the *Book of Lismore*, thus: "She is the prophetess of Christ; she is the Queen of the South; she is the Mary of the Gael." [9]

In one important respect the mythology is absolutely right. The old archetype, the universal feminine principle was indeed the 'midwife,' for the Incarnation is not only the fulfilment of the Old

Testament hope, it is the fulfilment of the entire religious quest of mankind.

We must return to the historical Brigid, however. She is fairly reliably believed to have been born some five miles from Kildare, of parents of humble origin, and to have been baptised by Patrick himself. She is believed to have become a nun at an early age, to have founded the famous monastery at Kildare and to have made a notable contribution to the spread of the Christian Faith in Ireland. She is patron saint of poets, blacksmiths and healers and the date of her death at the age of eighty-seven, is believed to have been 525.

We may see, in the mythology surrounding this Christian saint, something of the manner in which the new Faith affirmed, assimilated and fulfilled that which was best and truest of the old. This is a feature of Celtic missionary work, it echoes the approach of St Paul in Athens, when, taking the trouble to find out something of the religion of the Greeks to whom he was to speak at the Areopagus, he used their own poets and traditions as the starting point of his Gospel message. This demonstrates a Christian courtesy and respect for souls and it was blessed, in Ireland, by a remarkably speedy, and apparently peaceful, widespread acceptance of the Christian Faith as the fulfilment of the fundamental pagan religious hopes.

# A Revival of Baptismal Grace

Patrick's *Confession* is maddeningly imprecise about sequences of events and omits to make mention of a great deal about which we would wish to be better informed. He tells us that until the age of fifteen, when he was abducted, "I did not know the true God." This sounds improbable from one with a deacon for a father and a priest for a grandfather. It sounds very much more like the testimony of one who had been a nominal, and rather casual, believer and who had then undergone a profound conversion experience. It is not uncommon for such persons to deny that they had been Christian believers at all before that experience. Patrick would almost certainly have been baptized in infancy for the baptism of the children of Believers was common throughout the Church from the Third Century.

One thing is clear, however; Patrick experienced what theologians would describe as a revival of Baptismal Grace in Ireland. He testifies to his fervent life of prayer during his time as a slave, and there is an Irish tradition that he was indeed baptized during his period in bondage by one of the Candida Casa community, Caranoc, one of the first of that community to work in Ireland. This is by no means impossible, if Caranoc was a young priest at the time, for he spent much of his ministry in Ireland in later life. Some believe him to have been the immediate successor to Ninian at Whithorn, but this is uncertain.

It is claimed of Caranoc that he was the one who introduced the Celtic monastic-episcopal system into Ireland, though others, such as Finnian of Clonard, have similar claims made for them. This was a considerable departure from the continental-style diocesan episcopate that Patrick was seeking to establish but, being more immediately suited to the circumstances of Irish society, it quickly prevailed and, within a generation or so, seems to have been the norm.

By the mid Sixth Century, there were 'parishes' of monastic institutions, founded by, and owing allegiance to, a single prominent founder. We shall encounter this in a later chapter when we return to Ireland to make a study of Colmcille, initially at least the most determined 'empire builder' of them all.

The work of the Candida Casa mission in Ireland is much neglected. From their earliest involvement it seems clear that they sought to make contact with the pockets of Brythonic Celtic-speaking people in the south-east of Ireland. When Patrick finally arrived to begin his life's work in Ireland it is reported that he met the then much older Caranoc and they agreed that Patrick should work "to the left" and Caranoc should work "to the right." Left meant South and right meant North, where the Candida Casa mission was already established. Patrick ended up some way to the north himself, however, the site most certainly associated with him being Armagh in Ulster.

Patrick died in 461 but the exact date of his death, and the place of his burial, are not known for certain. There is a tradition that a grave at Glastonbury, of 'Patrick the Older,' is that of Patrick himself but this is unlikely. Eight ancient English churches were dedicated to Patrick, as were numerous chapels in Dyfed (Pembrokeshire). The Normans, who made incursions into Ireland some centuries later, encouraged his cult which is now widespread.

Though by no means the single-handed evangelist of the whole of Ireland in his own lifetime that popular enthusiasm portrays, he was, and remains, such a towering figure as to eclipse the multitude of fellow-evangelists from Whithorn and elsewhere whom he must have known and must have worked with. But Patrick, the "rustic," went to the top of society and converted the kings, the princes and the petty rulers. This was the key to the undoubted evangelisation of Ireland in two or three generations, corresponding closely to Patrick's own life span.

1  *Selections from Ancient Irish Poetry* (Kuno Mayer, 1928)
2  *Saint Patrick*, ed. Iain MacDonald (Floris Books, Edinburgh, 1992) pp.31-32
3  ibid. pp.35-36
4  ibid. p.45
5  ibid. p.13
6  ibid. p.17
7  ibid. p.21
8  *Saint Bride*, ed. Iain MacDonald (Floris Books, Edinburgh, 1992) p.27
9  ibid. p.10

## *chapter five*

# The Age of Saints in Wales

*Gwarchod i mi fy nhraed ar dir tirion Cymru.*
*Guard for me my feet upon the gentle earth of Wales.*

HE SIXTH CENTURY corresponds, very largely, with the life-span of Gildas, the first historian of Britain, who is believed to have been born at Arecluta, in Strathclyde, in or about the year 500. For some reason, in his youth, he fled to Wales where he married and was widowed very shortly afterwards. He then entered the monastic community of Illtyd, of whom we shall hear more later, and journeyed first to Ireland and then to Rome in about the year 520. Exact dates cannot really be determined but his early years would appear to have been nothing if not eventful.

Gildas was back in Wales in 527 and some sources claim that he had founded a small monastic community in Brittany in the meantime. Brittany was in a state of considerable flux at this period in history, for the relentless pressure of the Anglo-Saxons in southern Britain had caused a steady flight of displaced Celtic Britons from the south coast across the sea to what had been known to the Romans as Armorica, but which was in the course of changing its name to Brittany, as a result of this influx of refugees.

As we shall see, the British Church was to be much concerned for their spiritual welfare and several of those now revered as the Welsh Saints, of whom Gildas is one, spent a part of their lives in Brittany.

Gildas himself seems to have travelled, between his hermitage on Flatholm Island in the Bristol Channel, Ireland and Brittany, for the rest of his life. He is remembered chiefly for his historical work *De Exidio Britaniae* in which he paints a sorry picture of the corruption of native British rulers and blames their sins for the calamities which the Fifth Century had brought on the British people. He chronicles the various victorious battles against the Anglo-Saxons, fought by a leading British *dux bellorum* (war lord) by the name of Arthur, culminating in the battle of Badon (c.499). Following Badon, the Anglo-Saxon threat subsided and was not renewed until the middle of the century. Gildas died in Brittany in the year 570.

The life-span of Gildas corresponds not only with most of the Sixth Century, but also with most of what we might well describe as the Age of Saints in Wales. Wales in the Sixth Century was, for all intents and purposes, a Christian country with a well established Church. It was a part of a Celtic Britain which stretched from the Clyde to the south coast, following a line roughly equivalent to the Pennine Range extended both to the North and to the South, and which spoke essentially the same language, the forerunner of present-day Welsh. It was some fifty years before Gildas' birth, in the middle of the tormented Fifth Century, that a man was born who represents both a link with the Romano-British past and the Age of Saints with which this chapter is concerned.

# Dyfrig, direct descendent of Maxen Wledig

Magnus Maximus, the unsuccessful contender for the Imperial throne, and Helen, his wife, had a son by the name of Constantine. Confusion between two Empress Helens, each with a son called Constantine, is understandable but Constantine was a common name for boys at that time in Roman history. Constantine's own descendents included a grand-daughter by the name of Efrddyl, and she gave birth to a son whose Latin name was Dubricius, but whose

Welsh name was Dyfrig. Helen, Dyfrig's great-great-grandmother, was the one whose visit to the *muinntir* of Martin of Tours brought the idea of the monastic brotherhood as a tool for the evangelism of the rural areas into Britain. Wales was nothing if not rural and the emergence of an Age of Saints, so relatively few generations later, bears witness to the success of the *muinntir* which, in Wales, was often referred to as a *Llan*.

*Llan* is a word which is used for a church, but anciently the *Llan* was more than just a church building. It was more like a smallholding or small township of Christians, often surrounded by a wall or earth bank, which served as a centre for local evangelism. In true Celtic style, ancient churches and church sites bear the names of their founders, or the leaders of the larger communities under whose auspices they were founded. The names of churches and villages on the present-day map of Wales bear striking witness to the vigour of the Sixth Century Welsh Church.

Helen was a Monmouthshire lass and returned to her roots in her widowhood. Her descendent, Dyfrig, was Herefordshire born, at Madley, south of the river Wye and some six miles from present-day Hereford. We know very little of his early life except for legends that tell not only of an outstanding holiness, apparent from an early age, but also of a charismatic gift of healing. He is said to have presided, for seven years, over a *muinntir* at Hentland (Henllan), not far from the river Wye, and much later hagiographers give the improbable figure of a thousand clerics under his rule and guidance. We need not take the numbers too seriously. He moved his community to Mochros, the modern Moccas, and after some years seems to have crossed into Wales where we find him being described as a bishop, but there is no knowledge of how, or when, he attained to that dignity.

His links with the Age of Saints in Wales – and they were nearly all closely linked with one another – comes with a strong tradition that he visited the *muinntir* of Illtyd where he ordained Samson, another saint we shall encounter shortly, both deacon and priest. The two were to meet again, for Dyfrig was in the habit of spending Lent in a *muinntir* founded on an island by Pyr. This is almost certainly Caldey Island, the Welsh name for which is Y Byr. Samson joined this community and, upon the death of Pyr, Dyfrig appointed him Abbot. He also consecrated Samson bishop on 22nd February 521.

Dyfrig spent the last days of his life on Bardsey Island (Ynis Enlli) and died there, probably in the year 522. Six hundred years later his body was brought to Llandaff and interred, with great pomp and ceremony, in the Cathedral. Such was the veneration accorded to Dyfrig that the Cathedral was then taken down and rebuilt in order to be a worthy final resting place for a Saint whose holiness was legendary although so comparatively little is now known about him.

# The Influence of Illtyð

There are conflicting traditions about the early years of a man who was to have a profound influence on many well known names in the Age of Saints. Illtyd, according to one account, was a Breton, born in the year 425 and a disciple of Germanus of Auxerre who is said to have ordained Illtyd priest at the age of twenty-two, not long before he died. A completely conflicting tradition has it that he was a soldier and came to Glamorgan with his wife Trynihid. Influenced by Cadog, whom we shall meet shortly, he parted from his wife and entered upon the monastic life. Trynihid became a nun and founded her own *muinntir*. Her name is commemorated at Llantriddid and possibly in two other places. Confusion is worse compounded by a tradition that makes the year of Illtyd's birth 475 and not 425. The difficulties of pre-Dionysian chronology are well illustrated in his case.

Illtyd is mentioned in several *Lives* of Saints of this period. He first appears in the *Life of St Samson*, then in the *Life of St Paul Aurelian*, the *Life of St Cadog* and finally in the later *Life of St Illtyd*. Certain it is that he settled, and founded a *muinntir*, at Llantwit Major (Llanilltud Fawr) which became probably the most influential monastic settlement in Wales.

The word *muinntir* is preferred to the word monastery, at this stage, because the latter carries with it later mediaeval associations and styles which can mislead us. There was no formal school, as in later monasteries; they were not places of learning, other than that profound inner learning that comes from a life dedicated to prayer and the reading of the Scriptures. The Italian, St Benedict, roughly contemporary with Illtyd, describes a monastery in his Holy Rule as "a school for the service of the Lord." The word 'school,' in this context, does not simply denote a place of formal study, but rather a collegiate (or community) life to that end. Illtyd and Benedict would be in agreement in this respect although the styles of their respective communities would, quite possibly, have differed very considerably.

By this time the *muinntir*, as a tool for the evangelisation of the rural communities, was just beginning to give place to a more formally monastic institution. They were places that men came to – sometimes having been placed by their parents while still boys – to live the life of prayer with brethren. But they were also places that men went out from, having discovered the next call within their vocation.

Llantwit Major saw a number of great 'names' come and go over the course of the years, although Illtyd himself seems to have remained at Llantwit Major for the rest of his life. The great Samson was given to Illtyd by his parents at the age of five and went on, in his adulthood, to a considerable pastoral ministry in Cornwall and Brittany. Gildas seems to have spent some time at Llantwit Major, as does Paulinus (St Paul Aurelian) and Dewi (David), to whom we shall return in a later chapter.

There are conflicting accounts of Illtyd's death but the most likely one has him dying at Llantwit Major, either in the year 505 or in 525. The chronological problem besets us both at his birth and at his death, but his influence on the Church in Wales, in Cornwall and in Brittany – and possibly also in Ireland – through his monastic brotherhood at Llantwit Major, was profound.

# Che Stronger Samson

One of the greatest of the Sixth Century Welsh Saints was Samson, born in about the year 480 in Dyfed, a part of South Wales that contains the counties of Carmarthen, Cardigan and Pembroke. *The Life of St Samson*, perhaps the earliest and fullest of the various *Lives*, tells us that his parents Amon and Anna had been childless for many years, but during a visit to a wise man for advice, Anna had a dream in which an angel told her that she would have a son whom she must call Samson and who would be "holy and a high priest before Almighty God."

In due course the child was born and was named Samson. From his earliest years he wanted to be a Christian priest. His mother was all in favour but his father opposed the idea strongly. However, after being warned in a dream that he was opposing the will of God, Amon consented and the boy was taken to Llantwit Major and presented to Illtyd. He was about five years of age.

This story bears all the marks of the hagiographer and its biblical origins are obvious. However, the practice of presenting small children to a monastery was already well known. St Benedict refers to it in his Holy Rule, and so the story is probably no more than an embroidered telling of what actually happened. Samson is reported as settling in quickly, learning the psalms by heart – the normal practice in communities at that time – and establishing a reputation for true holiness.

At the age of twenty four, in the year 504, Samson was ordained deacon by Dyfrig, and a year or two later, Dyfrig again ordained him priest. On both occasions, *The Life* tells us, a dove was seen hovering over his head by several persons present. True holiness brings out both the best and the worst in other people and two brothers, jealous of Samson, made an unsuccessful attempt to poison him, following which he left Llantwit Major and moved, with Illtyd's blessing, to join Pyr's community on Caldey Island.

There is an incident, recorded in the *Life*, which tells of a messenger arriving at the monastery with a request from Samson's father, Amon, that he come quickly, for he was on his deathbed. At Pyr's insistence, Samson went home where his dying father confessed to him a grievous sin of which no one else was aware. Samson absolved his father and *The Life* tells us that Amon made a remarkable recovery and went, with his five other sons, into a monastery. Anna, so it is said, went into a convent leaving only Samson's sister, the youngest of the family, still in the world.

Again we may suspect conventionally pious embroidery partially obscuring a real incident.

Samson succeeded Pyr as Abbot, but some eighteen months later some Irish pilgrims arrived on their way home from Rome. For some reason, and with Dyfrig's permission, Samson accompanied them to Ireland, remained there for some time and then returned to Wales, not to Caldey but to a cave near the river Severn where he and a handful of others tried to live the life of hermits. This experiment did not last long for he was summoned to a synod at Llantwit Major following which he was consecrated bishop, in 521, with a clear vision that the rest of his life was to be spent away from Wales, ministering to the needs of the people, first of Cornwall and then of Brittany.

*The Life* tells of all manner of wonders performed by Samson, both in Cornwall and in Brittany, where he set up his headquarters at Dol. Samson remained in Brittany for the rest of his life and died at Dol, at the age of eighty, on the 28th of July 560.

Like Patrick in Ireland, Samson established good relationships with the local rulers and also with Childebert, King of Paris. Three years before he died, Samson attended the Council of Paris and signed its decrees *Samson peccator episcopus* (Samson the sinner, bishop). He is reported as always carrying with him a hammer and chisel with which he inscribed a cross on all of the many standing-stones he encountered, 'baptising' it and claiming it for Christ.

# cadog, the wealthy monk

Chronological uncertainty confronts us again in the case of Cadog, son of Gwynllyw, eldest son of Glywys, who ruled over a great part of what is now Glamorgan and Monmouthshire. Cadog's mother was Gwladus, either a daughter or a granddaughter of Brychan, the ruler of what was later known as Brecknockshire. Some sources give c.450 as the date of his birth and others c.500, but in any event he was born into the nobility of South Wales. At the age of seven, Cadog was committed into the care of Tatheus of Caerwent to be educated. He remained with him until he was nineteen and it is Tatheus who is said to have baptised him in infancy.

Cadog felt called to the monastic life and was given some land by his uncle, Paul, who was the ruler of a district called Penychen. There, at Llancarfan, Cadog founded his community, and the *Life of St Cadog* tells us that "a great many clergy from all parts throughout Britain flowed eagerly, like a river, to Saint Cadog, that they might learn to imitate his wisdom and his actions, for he always cheerfully received all who were anxious to pay instant obedience to the commands of God, and gave themselves up to the study of the Holy Scriptures." Cadog and his Italian contemporary, St Benedict, were both convinced of the importance of a threefold life of manual work, study and prayer as helping to integrate the whole person, body, soul (or mind) and spirit.

After some years, Cadog and a number of his brethren travelled to Ireland where they established a community on the river Liffey, probably not far from the present-day Dublin, and remained there for three years before returning to the monastery at Llancarfan which was found to be in a ruinous state. The place was restored and remained Cadog's base of operations for the rest of his life. While he was there, Cadog succeeded to all his father's lands and found himself doubling as both monk and the ruler of a wide area from the river Thaw to the Usk. He left behind him an enviable reputation as a wise and generous ruler as well as that of a holy monk.

Cadog was accustomed to spend Lent on Barry and Flatholm islands in the Bristol Channel but would return to Llancarfan on Palm Sunday in time for Holy Week and Easter. He was a great traveller according to the *Life*, which has him in both Rome and Jerusalem, but this may be more in the way of pious embroidery than historical fact.

He did travel to Brittany, however where he founded a community on the island known as Île Cado, and there are a number of ancient Breton churches dedicated to him, indicating an active life of evangelism and pastoral care.

In Wales itself, church dedications indicating, in the Celtic tradition, a foundation by the saint to whom they are dedicated, are to be found plentifully near Llancarfan in the Vale of Glamorgan.

There are more around Llangattock-nigh-Usk in Gwent, others along the various Roman Roads leading north and west, and others near Brecon, in the Towy Valley, in Gower, at Llawhaden in Pembrokeshire, and there was a Llangadog as far away as the parish of Amlwch in Anglesey.

*The Life*, written in the Twelfth Century by Lifris, Archdeacon of Glamorgan and "Master of St Cadog of Llancarfan," claims that Cadog spent seven years in Scotland; the church at Cambuslang is certainly dedicated to a Cadog but it seems more probable that this is the foundation of another local saint with the same name.

Cadog's monastery at Llancarfan was an important seat of learning until the time of the Norman Conquest. After the Conquest it became subordinate to the Monastery of St Peter in Gloucester (the present-day Gloucester Cathedral). The date of Cadog's death is unknown, as is the place of his burial. His feast is observed on the 24th of January.

# paulinus, or st paul aurelian

We cannot be absolutely certain that the Paulinus who was a pupil of Illtyd, along with Samson, Gildas and David, was the same Paulinus who Rhigyfarch speaks of as having been David's teacher. The name Paulinus (Paul) was a common one among Christian believers in the Fifth and Sixth Centuries and we are obliged to rely upon a Breton monk, Wrmonoc, writing in the year 884, for most of our information. Indeed, it is by no means certain that Wrmonoc is not himself inadvertently confusing two men called Paulinus, one whose ministry was in Wales (which Wrmonoc had never visited) and one whose ministry was in Brittany. Such were the comings and goings between Wales, Cornwall and Brittany in the Sixth Century, however, that we may assume, with some caution, that Wrmonoc's Paulinus may have been the one person.

According to Wrmonoc, Paulinus was born, of noble parentage, in Brehant Dincat, almost certainly the modern Llandovery. There is a parish by the name of Llandingad in Llandovery which suggests that this is, in fact, the Brehant Dincat of the Fifth and Sixth Centuries. After overcoming a great deal of parental opposition, Paulinus was sent to Illtyd's monastery which, according to Wrmonoc, was first of all on Caldey Island before settling permanently at Llantwit Major. Among Paulinus' fellow pupils were Gildas, Samson and David. At the age of sixteen he left and, with two of his brothers, Notolius and Potolius, he established a hermitage on some land belonging to his father, almost certainly at Llanddeusant in Carmarthenshire. Paulinus was ordained priest (we know not by whom) and it is said that he presided over a community of twelve priests, suggesting perhaps a Martin of Tours style *muinntir*, dedicated to rural evangelism as well as the communal life of prayer.

There used to be an annual fair at Llanddeusant on what was once observed in Wales as St Paulinus' Day, 10th October. Not far away, in the parish of Llandingad, there are two chapels dedicated to Paulinus, at Capel Peulin and at Nant y Bri, and a holy well bearing his name (Ffynnon Beulin). The only other church in Wales to bear his name is at Llan-gors. Here there are two chapels, one called Llanbeulin and the other Llan y Deuddig Sant (Church of Twelve Saints). Who were the twelve saints? They were almost certainly the twelve priests who were the companions of Paulinus.

Wrmonoc then deals with Paulinus' work in Brittany, where he is remembered as St Paul Aurelian. But is this the same man? Wrmonoc is obviously convinced of it but Rhigyfarch in his *Life of St David* casts doubt upon it, as does *The Life of St Teilo* in *The Book of Llandaff*. David is recorded as spending time with Paulinus and it was while he was at Llanddeusant he met Teilo, who was already studying with Paulinus, "so that whatever secrets of the Scriptures were previously hidden from them they were able, by studying together, to understand." It was Paulinus who later on caused David to attend the important synod of Llanddewi Brefi, and Teilo's own community, at Llandeilo Fawr, was no great distance from that of Paulinus.

Is Wrmonoc correct in identifying this Paulinus with St Paul Aurelian? There is a considerable confusion of feast days. 10th October is, properly, the feast of St Paulinus of York, not of Wales.

A Breviary of 1516 gives 12th March for the feast of St Paul Aurelian (with 10th October as a second celebration). But a Welsh calendar of the Sixteenth Century has 22nd November as "Gwly Polin, Escob," and the Church in Wales now commemorates St Paulinus on that day.

# The Age of Saints – Continued

We shall meet David, Teilo and Padarn in a later chapter, along with others from middle and North Wales. Welsh they all undoubtedly were, but we do well to remember that they were first of all Britons and that they belonged to that Romano-British Church which was founded in the context of the Roman Conquest of Britain and which had been left, by force of circumstance, to get on with its own faith and life in an isolation from the continent, and in particular from Rome which, though not absolute, was sufficient to preserve an essentially primitive Christian Faith, uncomplicated by the stresses, strains and questionable influences which were blowing about the Mediterranean world of the time.

It will have been noted, however, that the Anglo-Saxon pressure, westward across the Pennines, had been halted by the beginning of the Sixth Century. During a half-century or so of comparative peace, travel – to Ireland, to Cornwall and to Brittany – seems to have been commonplace, and a cross-fertilisation of ideas between the various Christian communities in these islands seems to have been both frequent and natural. These will remain features of note in the chapters that follow.

## chapter six

# A Very Hawk-Like Dove!

*A youth shall be born out of the North*
*with the rising of the nations;*
*Ireland shall be made fruitful by the great flame,*
*and Alba, friendly to him.*

Mochta of Lugbad

IXTY YEARS after the death of Patrick, on Thursday 7th December in the year 521, a Prince of the Irish Blood Royal was born, in Garten in Donegal. The boy's mother, Eithne, was eleventh in descent from Cathair Mór, King of Leinster. His father Fedhlimidh (pronounced *Phelim*) was a son of Fergus, son of Conaill Gulban, the son of Niall Noigaillach, the redoubtable Niall of the Nine Hostages, High King of Ireland from 379 to 404. By the laws governing these things in Ireland, the boy was fully qualified to be offered the throne when he grew to manhood, by virtue of his birth. These facts, carefully noted by his biographer, have considerable significance, for they imposed a burden of responsibility upon the young prince which was not shared, nor could be shared, by the great multitude of his Christian Brethren. They explain a number of puzzling incidents in his later life.

The boy was baptised by a priest called Cruithnechan, son of Cellachan, and given the baptismal name Colum (Dove). He appears to have also been known as Crimthann (Fox) but this may have been a family nickname for it is by his baptismal name that he is known. Indeed, it is by a nickname derivative of Colum that he is best known in Ireland, for the boy was devout from an early age and was forever to be found in the nearby church of Tulach Dubhglaise (Temple Douglas) and his playmates nicknamed him 'Church Dove' or Columcille, a name to which he answered to his dying day. It is interesting to note that Cruithnechan is a name derived fron *Cruithni*, the Irish name for the Picts. It is tempting to speculate that Columcille and his parents may have owed their Faith originally to that Whithorn mission to "the Irish Picts" of Ulster who were Brythonic Celtic speakers and who were to maintain a separate identity for two or three centuries to come.

# colmcille's education

Columcille was fostered with Cruithnechan, fosterage of both sexes being a common procedure at that time, and the fact that he was fostered on a priest indicates to us that Colmcille was intended for the priesthood, for a priest would not teach him the martial arts which was the normal responsibility of a boy's foster-parent and particularly so in the case of a boy of noble birth. Colmcille stayed with Cruithnechan for most of his schooldays but, "while still a youth" according to Adomnan his biographer, he went to the monastic school founded by Finnian in 540 at Moville, on the Strangford Loch. The influence of Whithorn on his life was therefore profound although there is no record of him ever visiting Candida Casa himself. While at Moville, at which he must surely have been one of the very first students, he was ordained deacon.

Still in deacon's orders, Colmcille moved on and the next stage in his education is significant, for he spent some time studying at the feet of an old man of Leinster called Gemman, described as "a Christian Bard." The bards and the druids had been of fundamental importance in Celtic pagan society and there is no reason for supposing that the bard was not of equal importance in Celtic Christian society. They were very powerful figures, wielding as much power then as does the popular press today. The Christian monk was fast supplanting the druid, for the Irish Church was by now organised tribally and thus fully integrated into Irish society.

It may have been for this reason that they consciously adopted the druidic style of tonsure rather than the Roman. Be that as it may, Colmcille, whose own bardic gifts were considerable, saw fit to learn his craft with a master. He was, after all, of the blood royal and his responsibilities would inexorably include the political as well as the ecclesiastical; he was a wise young man to recognise it.

Having concluded his bardic studies, Colmcille went on to the monastery of another Finnian, again a Leinster man, at Clonard in Meath where he was ordained priest by Bishop Echten of Clonfad. It was this Finnian, who had spent some time with Gildas of Wales, either in Wales or during one of Gildas' periods in Ireland, who was largely instrumental in replacing the Continental style episcopate with the tribally based system whereby the abbot of the (essentially tribal) monastery was the religious superior of the tribe. He might or might not be in episcopal orders himself. If not, then one of the monks of the community would be in episcopal orders, performing episcopal functions as and when required. This change of episcopal style was therefore in full progress when Colmcille was completing his time of formal education.

This formal education was now complete and so Colmcille set out with three friends to travel to Glasnevin (now a part of Dublin) where Berchan Clarainech (otherwise known as Mobhi), himself a former monk of Clonard, had established a monastery and school. Four more potent young men can seldom have been on a journey together; Colmcille himself was to go on to found the great monastery at Derry and a whole 'parochia' of monasteries before departing, in his early forties, for the work for which he is best remembered, on Iona. His companions are no less memorable.

Cainnech (Kenneth), born the son of a bard near Derry and a lifelong friend of Colmcille, went from Glasnevin to Llancarvan in Wales. On his return he founded a number of monasteries in both the North and the South of Ireland, the main foundation being that of Aghaboe in Laios, but other important foundations were those of Drumahose in Derry and Cluan Bronig in Offaly. Cainnech was also active in Scotland; there are churches in both Kintyre and Fife which claim him as their founder. Inchkenneth on Mull was his foundation, as was Kilchennich on Tiree and Kilchainie in South Uist. At Comcille's monastery on Iona, to which he seems to have been a frequent visitor, both a small church and a cemetery were dedicated to him. Cainnech also accompanied Colmcille on a journey to King Brude, the Northern Pictish king, at Inverness.

Ciaran mac Antsair, the son of a travelling carpenter of Connaught and nine years older than Colmcille, had been a monk under Enda on Aran island, where he was ordained priest. He had then spent time with another community on Scattery island before joining Finnian at Clonard. He was to go on to found the great monastery of Clonmacnoise (Cluan Mocca Nois) on the Shannon, where he died at the early age of thirty-three.

Comgall, to be known by later generations as Comgall the Great, the youngest of the four, founded the great monastery of Bangor in Ulster, the largest monastery in Ireland, which with its various daughter houses was to grow to a community of three thousand souls. He too was a lifelong friend of Colmcille and, in a tradition not wholly accepted by Colmcille's biographer, Adomnan, also accompanied Colmcille on a journey to King Brude at Inverness.

The year of the four's arrival at Glasnevin must have been 543 or 544, for they had not been there long before Berchan dispersed his community in order to avoid the Yellow Plague – almost certainly a bubonic plague – which had swept through Europe from Egypt, had decimated Constantinople and had ravaged Italy in 543. It was now making its appearance in Ireland, probably brought by rats in the trading ships from the continent.

# A Force to Be Reckoned with

The conversion of Ireland to the Christian Faith had been effected, as far as we are able to tell – and most unusually – without the martyrdom of any of the missionaries. There had been opposition in plenty, and we must suppose from the druids in particular, but there is no history of bloodshed. The Faith had been communicated most powerfully by the simplicity and holiness of life of those who manifestly lived the Gospel they preached. It seems to have been the case that they did not simply angrily confront and condemn the old religion so much as reveal some parts of it to be misconceived and, in any case, redundant in the face of the Incarnation. They then claimed all that was good and true about the rest, for Christ Our Lord came, as he said, "not to destroy but to fulfil." There was a total absence of 'churchy' triumphalism and the Faith had thus entered into, and had became incarnate within, the whole fabric of Irish society. It is probably true to say that by the end of the Sixth Century, Ireland was, nominally at least, a Christian country.

Several generations had passed since Patrick and his contemporaries and the Church was now, quite inexorably, involved in the political life of Ireland. A church leader's responsibility was to his people, his tribe. The authority of the Pope was largely an academic matter; he was a very long way away and communications were of the slowest. Papal authority does not seem to have been referred to in matters concerning Church life and discipline. The Papacy was not denied in principle, it was simply, and probably inevitably, ignored in practice.

We therefore find in Colmcille a very different type of ecclesiastic than Patrick or Ninian. What might seem to later generations and in a very different social context to be a form of empire-building, with the establishment of his own 'parochia' of monasteries, was entirely on behalf of, and for the benefit of, the people to whom he belonged and not in any way for his own glory. He, being of the blood royal, was also jealous for the integrity, political and religious, of Ireland as a whole. This should not be seen as diminishing his own undoubted sanctity, but it was to produce sets of circumstances, and contradictions, with which earlier evangelists had not had to deal and he must have experienced considerable difficulties with them, and not a little anguish, as will become clear.

By all accounts Colmcille had a commanding presence and a very powerful personality. Like any Celt, he could 'flare up', and during his bardic apprenticeship with Gemman an incident occurred which must have shaken both of them. They were walking in the country one day, and were for some reason some distance apart when a hysterical young woman ran up to Gemman, crying for protection from her pursuer. She fell at his feet and he cast his cloak over her, calling for Colmcille as he did so. Before Colmcille could get to her, her pursuer ran up and speared her to death through

Gemman's cloak. In righteous fury, Colmcille cursed the murderer with such vehemence that the fellow immediately fell dead with heart failure. One is reminded at once of the fate of Ananias and Sapphirah in the New Testament but such incidents are not usually reported of the Celtic Saints, over whom a later sentimentality has cast a rosy glow of a perpetually gentle piety. In reality they were decidedly flesh-and-blood real people, with all the quick temper, black-or-white opinions and ready remorse that are typical of the Celts to this day. Plaster statues they were certainly not!

Returning home to Ulster, Colmcille called upon his kinsman, King Aedh, and was given Daire Calgach (the oak wood of Calgach), a dun or royal hill-fort, as the site for his first monastery. The association with oak trees is significant; Colmcille is known to have loved them but perhaps he also held them in awe in consequence of their earlier druidic associations. What we now know as Derry was not only his first monastic foundation but also, having been a royal site, it was a reminder to one and all of Colmcille's royal associations.

The next fifteen years were taken up with the foundation of monasteries and the establishment of the *paruchia Columbae* which covered the territory dominated by Colmcille's family, the Uí Néill. His foundations included Derry, Durrow (another name, Dair Magh, referring to an oak wood), Clonmore in Co. Louth, Swords and Lambay in Co. Dublin, Drumcliffe and Drumcolumb in Co. Sligo, Moone in Co. Kildare and, possibly the most famous of them all, Kells in Co. Meath. The list is not exhaustive. They related to the local tribal kingdoms which, although nominally Christian, were frequently warring with one another, and together, to the Northern half of Ireland, ruled from Tara by the Uí Néill, as opposed to the Southern half which was ruled from Cashel by the Eoganacht.

It has to be admitted that, in many cases, the Christian Faith of some of the kings and chiefs seems to have been little more than skin deep and that they switched from druid to Christian priest and back again as the occasion seemed to demand. Colmcille had no illusions about the fragile hold of the Faith upon his people and acted swiftly, and fiercely, against anything that threatened its integrity or the integrity of newly founded Christian institutions. It is this that helps to explain the battle of Cúl Dreimne (Drumcliffe) in 561 and Colmcille's own part in it.

# The Battle of Cúl Dreimne

There is a popular tradition that the battle was the result of a dispute over a copy of the psalter, made by Colmcille in 560. During a visit to Finnian at Moville, Finnian claimed it. Colmcille claimed it as his own copy, the matter went to court and the King, Diarmait, ruled against Colmcille. Incensed, Colmcille raised an army and resoundingly defeated Diarmait in a pitched battle. As a result of the battle, which cost 3000 lives, Colmcille was exiled to Iona, with the task of converting 3000 souls to the Faith to replace the ones lost in a battle which was of his own making.

This tradition, whatever fragments of fact may cling to it, is manifestly unsatisfactory and quite unrealistic as it stands. The matter is very much more complicated than this and it has to do with the fact that Diarmait mac Cerbaill, when he became King at Tara in 560, was consecrated king according to orgiastic, pagan, druid rites – the Feast of Tara – although he was nominally a Christian. He then executed, at Tara, a young prince, Curnan, son of the King of Connaught, who had accidentally killed another young man during the sports which accompanied the Feast of Tara, and who was under the protection of Colmcille himself. This was a contemptuous breach of the fundamental monastic right of sanctuary. Diarmait also killed another prince of Connacht, Aed Guaine, who had sought sanctuary with Ruadan of Lorrha, himself another royal-born prince-monk, of the Eoganacht of Cashel. There is a tradition that the furious Ruadan pronounced a solemn curse upon Tara itself, and upon Diarmait personally.

Diarmait was of a Southern branch of the Uí Néill, with whom the Northern Uí Néill were in some rivalry. The King of Connacht was already on the march, to avenge the death of his sons and it would not need an outraged Colmcille to persuade the Northern Uí Néill to join forces in teaching Diarmait a sharp lesson. The armies met just outside Colmcille's monastery at Drumcliffe, under the southern slopes of Ben Bulben, and Diarmait, attended by his druids, was routed, with a great loss of life. Beyond doubt Colmcille was also there, performing for his own King a very similar function of prayer and protection that the druids were attempting to perform for Diarmait. This need not surprise us; it was the expected duty of the tribal abbot to so support his tribal king in battle.

Diarmait did not long survive his defeat at Cúl Dreimne. Tradition has it that he died very much as cursed by Ruadan and others. Certain it is, however, that Cúl Dreimne had an effect upon Colmcille. There is a suggestion that he was under some censure; even Adomnan hints as much, and two years later, in 563, he set out from Derry with twelve companions, to embark upon the 'white martyrdom' of exile – self-chosen in all probability – to begin the work for which, outside of Ireland, he is best known. He was then forty-two years of age.

# Dalriada and the Mission to King Brude

Romanticism has it that Colmcille and his twelve companions, having made an epic journey from Derry to Iona in a coracle, landed at Port-na-Churaich, buried their craft under a pile of stones and then climbed to the heights of the south-west corner of Iona to make sure that Ireland was properly out of sight. The name of that height is Càrn Cùl ri Éirinn, the 'Cairn of the Back-to-Ireland.' As always, the reality is more complicated and somewhat more prosaic for there was a decidedly political dimension to Colmcille's 'white exile' which is usually forgotten.

Sometime during the Fifth Century, warriors from the *Dal Riata* of Antrim, kinsmen of Colmcille, had effected a landing in Argyll and began the colonisation of that part of the Scottish mainland and nearby islands. They were, in fact, the first 'Scots' (Scotti) in Scotland, the Gaelic name for which is *Alba*. As they pushed further east and north, they came into collision with both the Picts and the Brythonic tribes of Strathclyde. Their King, Fergus Mór mac

Erc, established his capital on the rock of Dunadd and his territory was Kintyre and Knapdale. Fergus' brothers, Loarn and Aengus, settled Aengus on Islay and Loarn's territory was that which is now known as Lorn, centred on Dunally, not far from Oban. Bede, one of our sources of information, is unclear as to whether their arrival was contested or accepted peacefully by the existing population. Certain it is, however, that they were well established within two or three generations, if somewhat precariously.

The first king of a united Scottish Dalriada was Gabrain, a grandson of Fergus Mór, described by the historian Tigernach as *Ri Albann* (King of Alba). Perhaps it was the tensions suggested by such a title that provoked the king of the Northern Picts, Brude MacMaelcon, to march against these upstarts in 557 and resoundingly defeat them in a battle in which Gabrain was killed. Gabrain's successor, Conaill, is referred to as *Ri Dalriada*, suggesting that he owed homage to Brude. Colmcille, a kinsman of Conaill, would have felt a responsibility towards his own embattled folk in Alba and there is some evidence that he visited Conaill during the two years between the battle of Cúl Dreimne and his departure from Derry. Was it Conaill who granted him the isle of Iona? Was Comcille's subsequent visit to King Brude partly in order to confirm the arrangement?

We can only speculate on these matters. According to one tradition, Colmcille's first landfall, on his eventual voyage from Derry, was the isle of Oronsay, much closer to Conaill's territory, but, for whatever reason, he pushed on to Iona.

Colmcille's arrival on Iona is full of puzzles. The 'Old Irish Life' tells us that he was greeted by two bishops, resident on the island, but Colmcille saw that they were not true bishops and would not recognise them, whereupon they left the island to him. It is impossible to be sure what this story is all about. Other traditions have it that Iona was a druidic centre and that Colmcille chose it as his base of operations specifically for that reason and began by evangelising the druids! This would seem to be entirely in character with the man and, if successful, would be the shrewdest move of all in the matter of bringing the Faith to the Northern Picts. We do not know, but suffice it that Colmcille and his companions seem to have speedily settled down and to have established their monastery, and at some stage, a daughter monastery was established upon the isle of Tiree.

Bede tells us that the Picts were converted in 565. It is difficult to know what to make of this statement. The cleric who annotated the *Pictish Chronicle* (St Andrews MS) tells us that Colmcille converted Brude; other traditions have it that he also baptised him. Adomnan, however, shows Brude as adhering to the old religion and maintaining a pagan court, although, like his father, he tolerated and indeed was often kind to the Christians among his subjects.

Colmcille's visit to the court at Inverness was one of considerable importance and he appears to have been accompanied by his old friends of Clonard days, Cainnech and Comgall. That Brude had Christians (however few) among his subjects suggests the earlier influence of Ninian and his companions but the immediate purpose of the trio's visit was probably as much diplomatic as evangelistic. Colmcille's kinsmen of Dalriada were shaken and embattled and Colmcille needed Iona as a base, not only for local evangelism, but as a 'mother church' for Dalriada. Though Brude's conversion and baptism must be regarded as doubtful, the mission, in respect of its immediate diplomatic aims at least, seems to have been successful.

# Sτ Coluⴜʙα αɴᴅ Ioɴα

Adomnan, writing the biography of Colmcille a century after the latter's death, Latinised his name to Columba, the Latin for Colm, 'Dove.' It is by his Latin name that Colmcille is best known outside of Ireland, and St Columba and Iona have become inextricably interwoven one with the other, by the piety, and the romanticism, of later generations. The present mediaeval abbey is on the site of Colmcille's monastery and it acquired a new life and ministry during the second half of the Twentieth Century which would be an astonishment to its Sixth Century community.

That there seems to be something 'other' about the isle of Iona itself is the experience of multitudes of visitors over the centuries. It is a 'thin place' where, in Eliot's words, "prayer has been valid."

A pilgrimage that does not penetrate very far beyond the picture postcard trail from the jetty, the café, the gift shops and up to the Abbey and its impressive bookshop, may, in turn, not penetrate very far beyond a romantic vision of gentle St Columba, meek and mild.

There is practically nothing remaining of Columban date; even the great high crosses are at least two or three centuries later. It takes a great deal of imagination to remove the present ancient remains from mental vision and put in their place a scattering of beehive huts, made of whatever came to hand, an oratory or two, and the community chanting the psalms, and for all we know, celebrating the Eucharist (weather permitting) in the open air. An African Kraal would present every bit as impressive an outward appearance.

Colmcille's thirty-four years with Iona as his home-base turned the monastery into a veritable power-house of spirituality and learning. It became the mother-church, not only for the *Dal Riata* in Alba (the Scottish Dalriada) but also for the *Dal Riata* in Antrim (the original Dalriada).

Colmcille was a 'grey eminence' behind the throne of Dalriada and, in his time, he and his community seem to have evangelised at least from Ardnamurchan, south throughout Argyll, north-eastward up the Great Glen towards Inverness and eastwards into Athol. At a critical moment he intervened to consecrate Aidan as King of Dalriada and, on a famous occasion, met Kentigern, his British counterpart in Strathclyde and Cumbria, and exchanged pastoral staffs with him. Colmcille's political and diplomatic responsibilities never left him, and he never neglected them, but he was, first and foremost, a monk, an evangelist and a Saint of God.

Colmcille was a Celt through and through and he possessed the gift of 'sight' which is by no means rare in that naturally intuitive race. This gift of precognition is often feared, lest it chance to prophesy the unpleasant, but Adomnan's delight in recording many often inconsequental instances of 'the sight' in the life of Colmcille can strike the modern mind as extraordinary, even perplexing. Extraordinary it may be, but it is not necessarily incredible simply because it may not have been personally encountered or understood.

There was an occasion when Colmcille prophesied to some companions that a certain young monk would accidentally drop a valuable book in a bucket of water within a few minutes. This he did! On another occasion Colmcille cancelled a fast-day the evening before because they would have an unexpected visitor in the morning and it would be inhospitable to subject him to a fast after a long journey. The unexpected visitor duly arrived. This presents no difficulties to me as I have known, over the course of years, of a number of comparable, and not very consequential, examples.

More remarkable were the instructions given by Colmcille to one of his monks concerning a crane. The bird would land on such-and-such a beach in the morning. It would be completely exhausted and was to be taken in, fed, watered and generally cared for, for three days. It would then fly back to Ireland. To the astonishment of the community, everything happened exactly as foretold.

Profounder incidents include the stilling of two storms at sea. A bad storm overtook Colmcille's boat on one of his many sea crossings. He was baling out as vigorously as the rest when one of the rowers told him he could be better employed. They would see to the boat, he should emulate our Lord on the Sea of Galilee, and command the storm to be still! Colmcille meekly complied, stood in the prow of the pitching craft and spread his hands over the sea in prayer. The wind dropped almost at once and the rowers were suitably awe-struck.

A far more interesting example of storm-stilling took place on another occasion of great danger. Colmcille had begun his prayer and then suddenly stopped. "No," he said, "this storm is for Cainnech to pray for!" Some time later they learned that Cainnech had been about to dine in his monastery when he suddenly rose from table and cried out, "This is no time to dine! Colmcille is in danger!" He ran to the oratory and, such was his hurry, he lost a sandal on the way. A little while later he emerged, rescued his lost sandal and said, "Colmcille is safe; the storm is stilled!" Whereupon he returned to his meal. At sea, the wind suddenly dropped and the rowers heard Colmcille laugh and say, "Well done, Cainnech! Even though you did lose a shoe over it!"

To many, this story will seem entirely incredible, but not to me personally, having experienced more than one occasion involving being-in-two-places-at-once vision and communication, in the context both of great peril and of prayer. Rare though such occasions may be, they do happen, but they are *given*, they are decidedly not to be sought after.

The life of Grace is one of the transformation, even the transfiguration, of the total person. During this life-long process, in a life totally given to God, the natural attributes are turned from their negative aspects to their positive, and that which is of nature, such as the psychic gifts of intuition and precognition, are transformed, by the Divine Grace, into the truly spiritual. This process is visible in the case of Colmcille who was transformed from the dedicated but quite frightening priest-monk of the time of Cúl Dreimne into the entirely lovable and Christlike man that he became towards the end of his life. The druid in him became the Christian mystic.

At the beginning of his seventy-fifth year, Colmcille had a vision of angels and the clear and welcome understanding came to him that his time on Earth was drawing to its close. We should not romanticise this, or try to explain it away. Colmcille was entirely unconditioned by Victorian stained glass and pious picture-books. Angels are, as their name implies, 'messengers of God' and Colmcille recognised what his inner sight presented and he understood its message. Adomnan, who was born thirty years after Comcille's death, and succeeded as Abbot of Iona in his late forties, in 679, paints a very attractive picture of the Saint's last days. He bade a fond farewell to his old horse, thanked it and blessed it. He gave instructions as to who was to succeed him as Abbot; he gave instructions about his own burial and concerning who was to complete the copying of the Holy Scriptures that he would leave unfinished. He left everything tidy!

Colmcille died on the 9th of June 597. That very same year Augustine, sent from Rome by Pope Gregory, landed in Kent. His instructions included the bringing of the Celtic Church of Britain into line with Rome and receiving the submission of its Bishops.

## chapter seven

# Dewi Sant, Patron of Wales

HE PATRON SAINT of Wales was, in all probability, the child of a rape victim. One source gives the date of his birth as 462 but this is almost certainly wrong. Other sources give a more realistic date of between 495 and 500 and even this may need some revision if the date of his death is 601, as some sources claim, and not 589, which is by far the most likely. The chronological problem is ever present, but a life span of between 500 and 589 would seem to be the most credible of our options.

David's mother is generally agreed to have been a woman by the name of Non, a Virgin of Christ, who was raped, or at the very least seduced, by Sant, a prince or local king of Ceredigion. A kinder interpretation of events would see Non as having become a monastic later in life, but there does not seem to be any suggestion that she was ever Sant's queen. David's name in Welsh, Dewi Sant, thus refers to his father's name; it is not 'Saint Dewi' which is its expected – and perhaps more appropriate – meaning.

All this is what might be described as the received wisdom concerning Dewi's birth, but there is another possibility which, in my view, makes somewhat better sense. It is that it was Dewi's father whose name was Non. This is the same name, without diminutives, that was borne by Ninian. It is a man's name. There is in any event something improbable in the name 'King Saint (Sant) of Ceredigion' and if Dewi's parents were devout believers, this would make the scattering of foundations called Llannon in Pembrokeshire and Cardinganshire attributable to a devout local monarch, and "Dewi Sant" would be able to relax into its more expected meaning of "Saint David."

The exact circumstances of Dewi's conception and birth are very largely a matter of conjecture, however, as are most of the details concerning his life, for *The Life of St David* was written some five hundred years after his death, by Rhigyfarch, son of Sulien the Wise, Bishop of St David's from 1072 to 1085. It is a decidedly hagiographical document and much of its content is manifestly, even wildly, unreliable. Nevertheless, enough can be gleaned from this and from other sources to give us a picture of an undoubtedly holy man whose influence was profound in his lifetime and who is the only one of the Sixth Century Welsh Saints to have been formally canonised by the Western Church.

# Dewi's education and early Life

Dewi was baptised by Aelfyw, Bishop of Mynyw and was educated at Hen Fynyw in Cardiganshire, where Rhigyrarch tells us he learned to memorise the Psalms, the Collects, Epistles and Gospels for the whole of the Church's year and also the Creeds. He does not seem to have learned to read and write, however, if we are to believe Rhigyfarch, until he went on to study under Paulinus, where, we are told, he met and befriended Teilo, during which time he was ordained to the priesthood. Rhigyfarch then has him going off to found ten monasteries.

For 'monasteries,' we are probably wise to understand them as small communities, perhaps of a handful of like-minded people, who lived the life of prayer together and evangelised, and served the folk in the surrounding countryside. They survive today in place names like Llandewi of which the present parish church will be found to be dedicated to St David. This is firmly in the evangelistic and pastoral tradition of Martin of Tours.

There are good reasons for believing that one of the places Dewi visited on his travels was Whithorn in Galloway. There is a tantalising possibility that the Vallis Rosina, or Vale of Roses, where he founded the *muinntir* which now bears his name (St David's) has been confused with a name given, by the Irish, to Whithorn: *Ros-Nan*, or the Headland of Ninian. While at Whithorn, Dewi spent some time in St Ninian's cave at Glaston, and this may well explain Rhigyfarch's otherwise preposterous suggestion that he was the founder of Glastonbury Abbey in Somerset!

Rhigyfarch is a confused and confusing biographer. According to other sources, to which we have already referred, Dewi, Paulinus, Samson, and just possibly Teilo, were all disciples of Illtyd at the same time and it may well have been then that he was ordained to the priesthood. This seems to be a much more likely interpretation of events. Dewi and Teilo certainly met when studying with Paulinus at Llanddeusant, but the timing of all this is uncertain.

The three *Lives*, of Dewi, of Teilo and of Padarn, have them all going to Jerusalem and all being consecrated Bishop by the Patriarch and, according to Rhigyfarch, David being made Archbishop! The journey itself, though highly unlikely, is not impossible; however, there are political reasons for its invention in the Eleventh Century when the *Lives* began to appear. Soon after the Norman Conquest the claims of Canterbury over the Welsh Church were beginning to be asserted. If St David could be represented as having been consecrated bishop, and appointed archbishop, by no less a person than the Patriarch of Jerusalem, what claim could Canterbury possibly have over the Welsh Church?

A journey much more reliably known to have been made by Dewi was to Brittany, probably in 547, to escape the Yellow Plague. Tradition has it that he took his widowed mother with him and she died and was buried there.

# Dewi's Monastery at Glyn Rhosin

It was after his great labour of founding churches and monasteries that Dewi came to the place which has, forever thereafter, become associated with him and now bears his name. In Latin, the name of the place is Vallis Rosina, or Vale of Roses; Glyn Rhosin in Welsh.

This is a wondrous misnomer for the place is wild, bleak and rocky. However, the Welsh for a moor is Rhos, and this is the more likely original description. There is an ancient farm, Rhoson, nearby which might support such an assumption. We now know the place of Dewi's monastery as St David's but a doubt must remain over its original name for Ros-Nan, the Headland of Ninian, suggests some hagiographical confusion, not to mention romanticism, over the "Vale of Roses!"

Dewi did not settle immediately at St David's, Pembrokeshire, but first of all he began to organise his community at Old Mynyw, or Hen Fynyw, near Aberaeron in Cardiganshire, four miles from which is a church of Llan-Non, bearing his mother's – or perhaps his father's – name. Not long afterwards, however, he moved to a site that was to be permanent. Dewi's monastery was close to the sea but invisible from it. This was a wise precaution in view of the piracy with which the Welsh coast was constantly afflicted. The suggestion has been made that Dewi's monastery became, amongst other things, an outpost of Welsh language and culture in a corner of Wales which was, for a time, virtually under Irish occupation. This is not by any means improbable.

Life in Dewi's monastery is known to have been austere and apparently more so than at other Welsh monasteries, for the Desert Fathers were his model and his own life was the most austere of all. Dewi had long since earned himself the nickname Dyfrwr, or 'the waterman' because he would never drink anything but water. Rhigyfarch gives us a colourful account of the austerities of the place and the long hours spent in prayer but we must beware of the tendencies of hagiographers, writing centuries later, to romanticise austerity and long prayers as things undertaken almost for their own sakes and necessarily indicating extreme holiness. Disciplines, however, are means to an end; they become mischievous when they are allowed to become ends in themselves.

Nobody is likely to have been clearer about that than Dewi, a gentle holy man with both feet set very firmly on the ground. Perhaps it was the austerities of the community that provoked an unsuccessful attempt by two monks to poison Dewi. More probably it was his true holiness provoking an extreme reaction from their own inner disharmonies. At any rate, he survived it.

Various sources tell of a Synod of the Welsh Church at Brefi. Rhigyfarch tells us that its purpose was to deal with a revival of the Pelagian heresy but this is almost certainly wrong. It is more likely that its aim was to take steps to reform the morals of both clergy and laity which appear to have been is some disorder. Dewi was not inclined to attend but, at the suggestion of Paulinus, he was fetched by Dyfrig and Deiniol and spoke with an authority which commanded great attention and respect. Rhigyfarch, writing at the end of the Eleventh Century and always keen to fight off the determined claims of Canterbury over the Welsh Church, maintains that, at Brefi, Dewi was proclaimed Archbishop and that, forever thereafter, the Bishops of St David's would be the Archbishops of Wales.

This is delightful nonsense. Certain it is that, after Brefi, Dewi was accorded what we might describe as a primacy of respect.

Dewi died on Tuesday 1st of March 589. His feast has been kept on that day from earliest times. An Irish martyrology of c.800 records it on that date and Archbishop Chichele of Canterbury, who had been Bishop of St David's from 1408 to 1414 before his translation, ordered the feast to be kept on 1st of March in the Province of Canterbury (it was not kept, however, in the Province of York).

# Teilo of Llandaff – or not?

We have met Teilo already. He was a contemporary of Dewi and met him, certainly when they were both studying with Paulinus, but possibly at Illtyd's monastery earlier on. There is less certainty that Teilo himself was with Illtyd at Llaniltud Fawr (Llantwit Major) with Dewi and others. He is said to have been a pupil of Dyfrig before going on to study under Paulinus.

Teilo was born near Penally in Pembrokeshire, the son of Ensic and his wife Guenhaf, daughter of Liuonui. After completing his studies with Paulinus he is said to have accompanied Dewi founding churches and monasteries and to have lived with him for some time. *The Book of Llandaff*, drawing heavily on Rhigyfarch's *Life of St David*, has the two of them, with Padarn, journeying to Jerusalem and all three being consecrated bishop by the patriarch.

Llandaff has long claimed Teilo for itself and so the *Book of Llandaff* insists that Teilo was made Archbishop, and not David! As this whole journey to Jerusalem is almost certainly a hagiographer's fantasy we can discern herein a certain rivalry between the mediaeval dioceses of Llandaff and St David's!

The Yellow Plague of 547 caused Teilo and some companions to travel to Brittany. There he renewed acquaintance with Samson whom he had met when he was a pupil of Dyfrig. Teilo is the patron saint of the church of Landeleau where, according to legend, he rode the bounds of the parish on the back of a stag. There are a number of windows and statues in Breton churches showing Teilo and his stag.

When the Yellow Plague subsided, Teilo returned to Wales and lived the rest of his life as a monk, almost certainly at Llandeilo Fawr in Carmarthenshire, from where his cult spread throughout South Wales. It is Llandaff, however, that has claimed him for its own and for centuries it was thought that Llandaff was his monastery and not Llandeilo Fawr.

When Teilo died, legend has it that three churches claimed his body. Penally claimed it as the place of his birth and the burial place of his ancestors. Llandeilo Fawr claimed it because that is where he had lived and died. And Llandaff claimed it "on account of its having been his episcopal see, of its privileges and dignities, its consecrations and obedience and of the unanimous voice of all the diocese, and especially because of its former state, and the appointment of St Dubricius and other fathers." So states the *Book of Llandaff*, with sublime pomposity. The dispute was settled, so legend maintains, by the miraculous 'cloning' of the body into three identical bodies! Thus each claimant was satisfied and Teilo is, supposedly, buried in all three places!

Teilo's dates are unknown, save that he was a contemporary of Dewi, and thus lived through the most part of that remarkable Sixth Century in Wales which produced such an astonishing harvest of holy and memorable men and women.

We must now attend to the third Saint who, in the fantasies of the hagiographers, made that memorable journey to Jerusalem to be consecrated bishop by the patriarch. Alas for Padarn, he was the only one of the three who was not made the Archbishop of Wales! His biographer clearly had no political axe to grind.

# paðaᵲn, aʙʙoc anð ʙishop

The Padarn (Latin name: Paternus) who was the supposed companion of Dewi and Teilo on their journey to Jerusalem has to be somewhat painstakingly disentangled from two other, Breton, contemporaries of the same name, Padarn (Peternus) of Vannes and Padarn (Paternus) of Avranches. An unknown cleric of Brecon Priory in the Twelfth Century sought to reconstruct a *Life* from a lost and half-remembered older *Life* written by Ieuan, a brother of that Rhigyfarch with whom we are now familiar. It is, inevitably, full of confusions, improbabilities and simple mistakes.

The probability is that Padarn, the son of Petrwn and the grandson of Emyr Llydaw, arrived in Cardiganshire from somewhere in the south-east of Wales. He obtained a grant of land between the rivers Rheidol and Clarach and there he established his monastery of Llanbadarn Fawr where he ruled as Abbot and Bishop for over twenty years.

Practically nothing is known of him other than that he and his community evangelised and faithfully served the surrounding countryside from the monastery, in the best traditions of Martin of Tours, although unlike Martin, he was a monastic rather than a diocesan bishop. The diocesan system was well established in Wales by the time of the Norman conquest and it may still have been operating in what was left of Christian England in the Sixth Century, but Wales and Ireland were both still essentially dependent upon a monastery-based episcopacy.

Padarn seems to have been more closely associated with Roman-British civilisation than many others among the Welsh Saints. If his own origins were from the east of the country, this might explain it. His foundations tend to follow the line of Roman roads; to the west,

Llanbardan Fach, Llanbardan Odwyn and Pencarreg. To the east, Llanbadarn Fynydd and Llanbadarn Garreg.

According to *The Book of Llandaff*, Padarn left his monastery in his old age and spent the last few years of his life on Bardsey Island, where he died and was buried.

Padarn's monastery of Llanbadarn Fawr survived until after the Norman conquest. It lost its independence in 1115 and became a cell of the Benedictine monastery of St Peter in Gloucester. Twenty years later it regained its independence but, within a century, it had disappeared altogether.

# Taking Stock of the Sixth Century

This chapter and the two which preceded it have found us arriving at the Sixth Century, by which time the Christian Faith, though always embattled, was nevertheless thoroughly established in society in forms that reflected the shape and order of that society and was thus able to serve it as adequately as possible. It will be worth our while to be reminded, briefly, of the shape and order of the Church up to the Sixth Century, of its worship, its resources and of the shape of the societies within which it existed.

Roman Britain was a town-centred society. The multitude of petty kings in their hill-forts, surrounded by their own tribes, had become 'civilised' and the Briton had become a Romano-Briton, reproducing to an increasing extent the lifestyles of Mediterranean Rome, as far as they could be reproduced in a Northern climate. Agriculture had become much more efficient and now the task of the country was to feed the towns, and also provision the large military establishment always maintained by the Romans in Britain.

A town-based diocesan episcopate was fairly quickly established and would have grown and spread slowly throughout the Roman occupation. In due time the 'bishop of' wherever it was became the chief figure of ecclesiastical authority, but there would have been little outward display; persecutions were always a possibility and so, until the reign of Constantine, the Church and its hierarchs would have kept a very low public profile. A college of presbyters surrounded the bishop but church buildings would have been few indeed until it was safe to build them openly. Worship would have taken place, for the most part, in private houses.

It is not altogether too fanciful to suggest that, although anything like a formal parochial system such as we know it now may never have emerged in Roman times, the 'country parson,' such, perhaps, as Patrick's grandfather, may have been a figure occasionally met with in a rural area, his ministry supplemented by itinerant presbyters sent out by the local bishop from the town. Needless to say, this is all very much a matter of conjecture. The task of evangelising and ministering to the *pagani*, the country folk, would have been a perpetual problem, and until the spread of Martin of Tours' new initiatives, a practically insoluble one.

Worship would have been centred on the Eucharist, expressing in word and deed the mystery of Christ, and in its celebration, turning a gathering of individuals into the Church. Copies of the Old Testament, and of the emerging books of the New Testament, would have been few and far between. Every copy was a hand-copy. Much of it was learned by heart – a feature of Muslim religious education to this day. The Church would have been an organism with an irreducible degree of organisation and thoroughly integrated into Romano-British society, within which it evangelised, quietly, by word, deed and by the quality of its life, both individual and corporate.

With the departure of the Legions and growing disorder, invasions and warfare, Christian Britain, by the end of the Fifth Century, seems only to have existed west of a line drawn down the Pennines, from the Roman Wall and extending down to the south coast. East of this line, in land now occupied by Angles, Saxons and Jutes, it is virtually impossible to say either what happened to the remaining Britons or what happened to the Church among them. There is some reason to suppose, however, that in the western half something approaching Romano-British Church order still obtained.

Wales, at the beginning of the Sixth Century, was part of Britain but as Roman occupation had been scanty compared with the rest of the country, there was very little urbanisation. Wales was still essentially tribal and rural and, in addition, it was mountainous. It was the evangelisation of rural Wales that Helen was thinking of when she made her momentous visit to Martin at Tours.

By the time we are able to discern a shape for the Welsh Church and the society it served it is plain that diocesan episcopate formed no part of it. The great *muinntir* of the Welsh Saints were presided over by an abbot in bishop's orders. Priests were consecrated bishop in order that they might go forth and evangelise, and thus create the Church in a new place. Monastic bishops were missionary bishops and they obtained grants of land upon which to build from the local petty king, successor to the tribal chief. From their *muinntir*, which we now call monasteries, they would set up new *muinntir* (families) to evangelise and serve the local communities. These are the *Llan* which, to this day, bear their names.

We are possibly misled by our use of the word monastery to describe these *muinntirs*. To be sure, all monastic communities are families, but the word has acquired a deal of baggage belonging to mediaeval times, most of it irrelevant to the Sixth Century. Of great stone churches, cloisters and monastic buildings, there were none. The monastic family lived in individual round huts within a banked enclosure. An oratory or two, built like the huts, of timber, wattle and daub, or whatever could be found, would not be big enough to take all the members of a large community and some, at least, of the worship would be offered in the open air. Study of the Scriptures would be largely effected by hand-copying and by memorisation.

It was all to do with life, and with the meaning of life, and with eternal life. And it was all to do with the integration of Earth and Heaven and the transfiguration of the former in the latter. Creation is blessed, the transfigured image of its Creator. There was no false dichotomy between the 'material' and the 'spiritual' which was to subtly pollute the Faith in centuries to come. The Faith of Sixth Century Britain, Wales, Scotland and Ireland was still the primitive Faith and the Church, though intelligently organised for its task of evangelism and pastoral care, was still essentially an organism. The great, towering – and sometimes stifling – Institution was yet to come.

# Tysilio, the Reluctant Prince

Brochwel Ysgythrog, the ruler of Powys, will provide a link between the next three Saints whose lives we shall now consider. One of his three sons, by Arrdun his wife, was Tysilio who was born in or about the year 575, at Pengwern (Shrewsbury).

From his earliest years, Tysilio wanted to become a monk but his father would have none of it; the boy must be trained as a warrior. One day, when out hunting with his brothers, Tysilio left them and fled to the *muinntir* presided over by Gwyddfarch at Meifod in Montgomeryshire. Brochwel flew into a rage at hearing the news and sent a detachment of soldiers to bring the boy back, by force if necessary. On their arrival, Gwyddfarch allowed them to see Tysilio, who appeared dressed as a monk. The soldiers' nerve failed them and they returned to Brochwel without him.

Fearing that Brochwel might come in person and force him to return home, Tysilio obtained Gwyddfarch's permission to leave Meifod and find somewhere safer for the pursuit of his vocation. He journeyed to Anglesey and gathered a Community about him at Llandysilio, near the Menai Strait.

After seven years, Tysilio judged it safe to return to Meifod. Gwyddfarch was now an old man, and after his death Tysilio succeeded him as Abbot. The community had grown and new building work was necessary to accommodate the brethren. While this was in progress, one of his kinsmen, Bueno, visited him for 'forty days and forty nights,' together with some of his own followers.

At about this time, either in 607 or 613, the Anglo-Saxons, under Ethelfrid, invaded North Wales and a terrible battle was fought at Chester. Brochwel is said to have led the Welsh forces and to have survived the battle, but died shortly afterwards. He was succeeded by one of his sons who also died, two years later, leaving no children. Tysilio's widowed sister-in-law then sent messengers to him reminding him of his secular duty. He must abandon the monastic life at once and come and marry her! This Tysilio politely declined to do.

It has been said that hell hath no fury like a woman scorned, and this became immediately apparent in the case of Tysilio's sister-in-law. Such was the injury which she sought to inflict on Tysilio and his monastery that he and a few of the brethren decided to leave Meifod and they journeyed to Brittany, where he spent the rest of his life.

Tysilio, known in Brittany as Suliac, died on 1st of October 650. He is buried in the church of St Suliac on the Rance. Tysilio's foundations in Wales, apart from Llandysilio in Anglesey, include other Llandysilios in Mongomeryshire, Denbighshire, Cardiganshire and Pembrokeshire.

# Bueno, a Shropshire Lad

Bueno was born in Shropshire, near the River Severn, in about the year 550. He was thus of an age with Tysilio, and being a kinsman of Mawn, another of Brochwel's sons and thus brother to Tysilio, was a kinsman, no less, of Tysilio himself. Bueno is said to have been the child, in old age, of Bugi and his wife Beren. He was educated at Caerwent, where Cadog had been educated before him, and his teacher was Tangwn who had succeeded Tatheus, Cadog's teacher.

Bueno remained at Caerwent until he was ordained priest. He had won the admiration and respect of the local king, Ynyr Gwent, who, among other favours, granted him some land, a township in a district called Ewyas, now Llanveynoe (Llan Feuno) in Herefordshire.

A few years later, Bueno's father became seriously ill. Bueno returned home and, after his father's death, he founded a *muinntir* on the land he had inherited, at the place now called Llanymynech. A legend has it that he planted an acorn on his father's grave which grew into a great oak tree. One branch grew down to the ground and it is said that any Englishman who passed under it would fall down dead! Welshmen, on the other hand, would be quite unharmed!

Bueno's next foundation was at Berriew, near Welshpool where Brochwel's son Mawn gave him some land. The invasion by the

Anglo-Saxons obliged him to leave and this was the occasion of his brief sojurn at Meifod, with Tysilio, before going on to Gwyddelwern, near Corwen, where they obtained some land from Cynan Garwyn, the local chief.

Bueno was a hot-tempered man and an incident occurred as a result of which he angrily cursed a badly behaved grandson of Cynan. The young man fell dead and it may have been this incident that caused Bueno and his companions to move on to Gwynedd, where Cadwallon had succeeded his father Cadfan as king.

Cadwallon gave Bueno some land in what is now Llanwnda parish in exchange for a gold staff worth sixty cows, and while Bueno and his companions were building their huts a young woman arrived, asking for baptism for her child. The child wept loudly and the young mother explained that the reason for its distress was that Cadwallon had sold Bueno the land that was rightfully its own inheritance. After baptising the child, Bueno confronted the king and accused him of dishonesty. Cadwallon refused either to exchange the land for some of his own, or to return the purchase price, whereupon Bueno cursed him and departed.

Bueno was followed by Cadwallon's cousin, Gwyddaint who, "for the sake of his soul and of the soul of his cousin Cadwallon," gave him his own land at Clynnog in Arfon. There Bueno built what was to be his chief *muinntir* and remained there for the rest of his life. He died on Low Sunday in or about the year 630. Bueno's name occurs more frequently in North Wales dedications than that of any other saint and it has been claimed that his missionary work is comparable to that of Dewi in South Wales.

Bueno clearly had a ministry of healing and there are many stories of him healing men and women whose heads had been cut off! This is probably a reference to them having "lost their heads" – in other words, their wits – as a result of some great trauma. He helped them recover their sanity. One of these was Winefred, daughter of Tefydd, son of Eiludd, who owned land in what is now Flintshire. Her mother is said to have been Gwenlo, a sister (presumably an older sister) of Bueno. Winefred was thus his niece. She was a Virgin of Christ, at Holywell, one of Bueno's foundations, after which she became Abbess of Gwytherin in Denbeighshire. She died on 22nd of June, somewhere between 650 and 660.

# Melangell, Virgin of Christ

If you leave Shrewsbury by the A5, driving north-west, and if you then keep a sharp look-out for the turn to the left on the B4396, and keep on that road, you will sooner or later cross the Welsh frontier at Pen-y-bont. When, after some distance, you reach Penybontfawr you will have to take the right fork, and continue on the B4391. This road would eventually take you over the Berwyn mountains to Bala and beyond, but for our present purpose you need follow it only as far as the village of Llangynog. Here, a tiny road branches off to the left and is signposted to Pennant Melangell. Pray to all the Welsh Saints that you meet nothing on that road because it is only one car's width, winding and steep-sided for most of its two miles. But when it widens out and you find yourself at the head of the Nant, or blind valley, something will tell you that you are but a stone's throw from Heaven!

It was just possibly this route – more or less – that the daughter of a Celtic chief followed when she rebelled against an arranged marriage with one of her father's friends. But that depends upon her being a British Celt from, let us say, Shropshire. There is, however, a strong tradition that she was Irish. The circumstances of her flight are the same. She fled from an arranged marriage because she felt a profound vocation to the eremitical life – that is to say, the life of a hermit. She settled in this idyllic and secluded valley, where nobody could possibly find her.

But she was found. In the year 604, the King of Powys, our friend Brochwel Ysgythrog, was hunting hares. He came to this valley and his hounds started a hare and chased it out of sight. When Brochwel caught up with his hounds he found them looking hungrily in the direction of a remarkably beautiful young woman who was obviously rapt in divine contemplation. As he looked, the hare peeped out from under her skirt. "Catch it!" he cried to his hounds, "Catch it!"

But, instead of seizing the hare, the hounds backed off and suddenly fled down the valley, howling. Brochwel was completely taken aback and, as the young woman was now finished with her prayer, he asked her what this meant. She told him that she had also been a fugitive and had found sanctuary in this valley, just like the hare! And she went on to tell him the whole of her story.

Brochwel was so touched by her words and evident holiness, and so astonished by the whole experience, that he gave the whole valley to Melangell then and there, to bear her name and to be, for her sake, and in the name of Christ, "a perpetual asylum, refuge and defence."

The little mediaeval shrine church, beautifully restored, is guarded by yews of such antiquity that Melangell must surely have known them. It is a place which will bring all but the most insensitive to complete silence, if not to their knees. She is buried in the tiny apsidal shrine behind the altar. Melangell is now regarded in Wales as the patron saint of animals and nature, and a society for animal welfare and nature conservation, established in her honour, bears the name *Cymdeithas Melangell*.

There remains a multitude of Welsh Saints of the Sixth Century whom we must pass over in our present study. Deiniol, son of Dunawd, founder of the great *muinntir* of Bangor Iscoed, was one of those who, with Dyfrig, persuaded Dewi to attend the Synod at Brefi. Cybi was the Abbot of Caergybi, or Holyhead. Oudoceus, or Dogo, was the founder of the *muinntir* at Llandogo in the Wye Valley. Gwynllyw, father of Cadog, somewhat of a "robber baron," was converted by his son and ended his days as a hermit.

There are many more but, in the next chapter we shall meet one of them: Asaph, in the context of his association with a great Saint of southern Scotland, Kentigern, otherwise known as Mungo (Munghu – "Dear Pet") and known in Wales as Cyndeyrn.

## chapter eight

# 𝕿he King's Grandson

HERE IS GOOD reason for supposing that Kentigern was the grandson of Urien, King of Rheged, a small but powerful British kingdom which included the whole of present day Ayrshire, and was born some time in the middle of the Sixth Century. As always, exact dating is impossible, and as we shall discover, particularly difficult in this period of conflicting scholarly opinion.

Kentigern's biographer was Jocelyne, a monk of Furness Abbey, writing about the year 1184. This is six hundred years after the death of his subject, and his *Life* is frequently both fanciful and romantic and care has to be taken to extract reliable details. We understand from Jocelyne, probably correctly, that Kentigern was an illegitimate child and was given into the care of Serf (Latin name Servanus) a monastic bishop and the apostle of Fife, for his education.

Serf had a school at his *muinntir,* which was situated at Culross on the north bank of the Forth, and the young Kentigern quickly became an especial favourite and was given the nickname Mungo (Munghu) which means "dear pet." It is by this nickname, Mungo, that he is known to this day in Scotland. Jocelyne tells us that Kentigern's fellow pupils became jealous of the special place he held in the old bishop's affections and so, when he felt confident enough to leave the monastic school, he did so. In due course, and apparently when still a young man, Kentigern was consecrated bishop and made his headquarters at one of Ninian's early foundations, at what is now Glasgow.

We know nothing of Kentigern's life between his leaving Culross and his consecration as bishop. He is said to have been a monk of the Irish tradition, and this probably means that either he gathered a community around him, or that he became first a member of a *muinntir* and then the natural leader of it. A Norman monk, writing six centuries later, would be quite likely to describe the monastic system of Kentigern's day as Irish and to make the mistake of supposing that his consecration in Glasgow was to a territorial diocese and not as a monastic bishop.

Jocelyne tells us that Kentigern's influence extended from coast to coast, south of the Antonine Wall, and describes his diligence in teaching the Faith to a population who, though nominally Christian, were plagued with heresies and false doctrines of all kinds. He claims that Kentigern was consecrated at the remarkably early age of twenty-five, which, though unusual, is possible. He goes on to tell us that he lived to the age of one hundred and sixty, which is not!

Kentigern is described as "of middle height, rather inclining to tallness." He was powerfully built and "beautiful to look upon, and graceful in form." His was a naturally attractive personality and "his outward cheerfulness was the sign and most faithful interpreter of that inward peace, which flooded all things with a certain contentment of holy joy and exultation, which the Lord bestowed upon him." And of his way of speaking it is reported that "he spoke in weight, number and measure as the necessary occasion demanded, for his speech was flavoured with salt suited to every age and sex. Yet the saint preached more by his silence than many doctors and rulers do by loud speaking, for his appearance, countenance, gait, and the gesture of his whole body, openly taught discipline and, by certain signs flowing forth, outwardly revealed the purity of the inner man." [1]

Jocelyne, who is capable of wild and improbable flights of pious, romantic fancy, sometimes comes down to earth splendidly and, in the passages quoted above, he has given us a vivid and very probably an essentially authentic picture of Kentigern, taken from the various sources that Jocelyne himself had used for the writing of his *Life*.

# The Arthurian Connection?

The historian Gildas, whom we have met in an earlier chapter, was born in Strathclyde, and for whatever reason, was forced to flee from it as a young man. He tells of a series of successful battles, fought against the Anglo-Saxons, culminating in the battle of Badon, following which there was a half-century of peace.

Other sources, including *The Easter Annals* of the *British Historical Miscellany*, give the victor of Badon as someone called Arthur. Thus the entry for what is probably the year 518 records the "Battle of Badon in which Arthur carried the cross of Our Lord Jesus Christ on his shoulders for three days and three nights and the Britons were victors." There is considerable argument concerning the actual date and place of this battle. Some scholars would put it as early as 490, but the fact of it, and its association with a British commander called Arthur, is not seriously in dispute.

*The Easter Annals* of the year 539 contain another reference to Arthur. They record "The strife of Camlann in which Arthur and Mordred (Medraut) perished. And there was plague in Britain and Ireland." It would be very tidy if the Plague could be identified as the Yellow Plague, but the dates seem to be against us. Plague, of one form or another was very probably a not infrequent scourge at that time in history.

The site of the battle of Camlann is uncertain except that it is almost certainly somewhere between the Antonine Wall and Hadrian's Wall, in southern Scotland. Medraut was the son of Loth, or Lot, the petty king of Lothian and the battle was part of an internecine strife between Britons. Once again, some scholars would push the date of the battle back to 510 but there is no certainty of dating at this period of history.

Our interest is aroused, however, by the appearance of names which are met with in the remarkable conflation of myths, legends, borrowings from the Welsh *Mabinogion* and strange tales which form the Arthuriad. The historical Arthur becomes a legendary king, somewhere in southern England, King Loth of Lothian becomes King Lot of Orkney and Loth's son, Medraut – Arthur's bane – is turned into Arthur's bastard son Mordred, born to the enchantress Morgana le Fay.

It must be remembered that Britain, a cluster of small kingdoms under a few, local over-kings, stretched, theoretically, from the south coast of England to the Antonine Wall. There was no separate Wales, or Cornwall. There was one B-Celtic language (doubtless with regional variations) and there was one essential culture. In this connection we may note that, to please the Norman French royalty and nobility of a later age, the Arthuriad as prepared by Geoffrey of Monmouth introduced a Breton (i.e. French) knight, Launcelot du Lac, as the all-time star of the Round Table!

What is the connection, if any, with Kentigern? Simply a charming, if doubtful, story that at some stage in his life he healed and baptised a Bard who had gone mad following the slaughter at Camlann and spent years wandering in the woods. The name of the Bard was Merlin, who was to figure, much later on, as the Wizard (druid?) at the legendary Court of King Arthur.

# Kentigern's Banishment and its Circumstances

Jocelyne tells us that "a certain tyrant, by name Morken, had ascended the throne of the Cambrian kingdom, whom power, honour and riches had persuaded to exercise himself in matters which were too high for him. But his heart was as elevated by pride as it was blinded and contracted by greed. He scorned and despised the life and doctrine of the man of God, in secret slandering, in public resisting him from time to time, putting down his miraculous power to magical illusion, and esteeming as nothing all he did." [2]

Jocelyne's vivid sketch of Kentigern's persecutor is authenticated from other sources and, indeed, the "Morken syndrome" is discernible and widespread in every generation from then until the present day. The main cause of the final breakdown in the relationship between Kentigern and Morken is given as a piece of Divine intervention in which the river Clyde overflowed its banks, picked up all Morken's barns, with the corn in them, and deposited them, bone-dry, on the lands of Kentigern's *muinntir*. We may enjoy the story but we are unwise to take it too seriously. The probable causes of the trouble go deeper than that.

The danger from the Northumbrian Angles brought several mutually jealous British kings into alliance against the common enemy. Hussa, son of Ida, was pushing north between the Tweed and the Forth and the danger this presented brought four British tribal kings into alliance. There were Urien, grandfather of Kentigern, Rhydderch, Gaullac and Morken. A few years later another son of Ida, "Deodric the Fire-Spreader," renewed the Anglian offensive northwards. He was opposed by Urien whose son Owain (Kentigern's natural father?) had, some years earlier, defeated Ida. Differences and rivalries between the British tribal kings meant that Urien was taking on the Angles unaided. Nevertheless, Urien was successful and the Angles were chased back south of the Tweed.

At some stage, possibly during his return, the aged Urien was stabbed to death by Morken, perhaps through jealousy at Urien's success. This may cast a better light upon Morken and Kentigern's attitude towards each other but the exact dating and sequence of events is very difficult to determine.

Whatever either the exact circumstances or the exact date, Kentigern was forced to flee Strathclyde, presumably with some at least of his companions, and according to Jocelyne he had determined to visit Dewi in Pembrokeshire. On the way he is known to have stayed for some time in Cumbria where several dedications point to his activities in that region. From Cumbria, Kentigern travelled to South Wales by sea and, after a mutually rapturous greeting, left Dewi, after a short stay, and made his way to what is now St Asaph's in North Wales, where he established his new *muinntir*.

It must be said that some scholars doubt that Kentigern ever got as far as Wales at all, never mind visiting Dewi. There is a notable absence of dedications to him in Wales, but the facts of the matter are that we do not know for absolute certain where he went, who he met or what happened, or even when. There is no reason, however, why the main outlines of Jocelyne's account may not have been accurate, even if the pious embroideries are discounted.

Kentigern, who is known in Wales as Cyndeyrn, gathered about him a community which Jocelyne would have us believe numbered almost a thousand brethren. Numbers, in these hagiographies, must be treated with great caution. There is a tendency to "add a nought" to any likely figure, just as the priestly authors of the Pentateuch thought nothing of adding a few noughts to some of theirs!

# Che Appearance of Asaph

Asaph, one of Kentigern's young companions in Wales, makes a brief appearance in Jocelyne's *Life*. As Kentigern was particularly beloved of his teacher, Serf, so Asaph was beloved of his superior Kentigern, who recognised his potential and his deep spirituality. Jocelyne tells of the young Asaph contriving to carry hot coals in the folds of his habit with which to supply a fire for Kentigern. He managed to effect this, by some means, without damage to himself or his habit and this, to Jocelyne, was miraculous.

Miraculous or not, Asaph was ordained at as early a date as Kentigern thought wise and was soon to have great responsibilities thrust upon him, for messengers arrived from Rhydderch, now king of Strathclyde in place of the ill-favoured Morken, inviting Kentigern to return and re-establish his *muinntir*, and take in hand the evangelism, all over again, of his own country. We are told that, at first, Kentigern was reluctant to leave Wales but concluded that it was the will of God for him and that he must obey.

Asaph was placed in charge of the *muinntir* in Wales and, we are told, a sizable proportion of the community decided to go north with Kentigern. The date of his return is as uncertain as the date of his exile but it is sometime in the last quarter of the Sixth Century. The rest of Kentigern's life and ministry was spent in his native Strathclyde. Glasgow Cathedral, built centuries later on the site of his *muinntir*, is dedicated to him in his nickname of Mungo.

It was probably early in the last decade of the Sixth Century that the famous meeting between Kentigern and Colmcille took place, at which they exchanged pastoral staffs. Kentigern was to outlive Colmcille by some fifteen years and died on the 13th of January in the year 612, although some sources give the date of his death as 603.

On, or near, the site of Kentigern's *muinntir* in North Wales, the Normans built a Cathedral, to be the seat of a territorial bishop rather than a monastic. Its first Norman bishop, Gilbert, was consecrated in 1143 and the Cathedral is dedicated to St Asaph.

There are a number of commemorations of Asaph in place-names, such as Llanasa, Pantasa, Ffynnon Asa and Onen Asa. Ffynnon Asa was a spring whose water was thought beneficial for rheumatism and nervous disorders.

# Che Division of Celtic Britain

The Yellow Plague of around 547 may very well have had a worse impact upon Celtic Britain than upon the Anglo-Saxons in that it appears to have come with shipborne rats from the Continent and from the Mediterranean in particular. These would naturally have arrived in the Celtic ports and not those occupied by the Anglo-Saxons, whose overseas connections would have been from southern Scandinavia and North Germany. This must be a matter of speculation but it may help to explain a resurgence of Anglo-Saxon expansion westwards in the second half of the Sixth Century. Indeed it has been suggested that they did not so much conquer as walk, unopposed, into many places which had been radically depleted of population or even emptied altogether by the plague.

Be that as it may, by the end of the century two thrusts to the West, one towards Bristol and the other towards Chester, were to effectively cut Celtic Britain into three disconnected pieces. In 577 a powerful force, the war-host of Wessex, led by Ceawlin and Cutha, inflicted a major defeat on the Britons at Dyrham, near Bristol. The towns of Cirencester, Bath and Gloucester fell into their hands and a bishop, Eldad (Aldate) was among the slain. It is possible that he was a territorial bishop, perhaps of Gloucester, as the territorial system seems still to have existed alongside the monastic in some parts of the country.

A generation later, in 613 (though some sources give 607, or even 616) a powerful Anglo-Saxon force thrust westwards from Northumbria and inflicted a serious defeat on the British at Chester. There was a great loss of life and Bede tells us that the invaders fell upon the great monastery at Bangor Iscoed and slaughtered twelve hundred of the monks, almost half the community. Again, we may wonder if a nought has been added to the figures, for the number seems less than credible even if the massacre does not.

By virtue of these two massive reverses, Wales was effectively isolated. It was cut off from Cumbria and the British tribal kingdoms up to Strathclyde, and it was also cut off from the South-West of Britain which gradually became Anglo-Saxon, with the proud and enduring exception of Cornwall.

This is a good point, coinciding as it does with the deaths of Kentigern and Dewi, to bring our study of the Celtic Saints of Britain to a close. But we have not done yet, for there are two further matters which demand our attention before we draw conclusions from our study. The first is the life and work of Maelrubha, the red haired apostle to the North-West of Scotland, and the other is the Celtic influence upon the Anglo-Saxons themselves, typified by Aidan, whose *muinntir* was established on the island of Lindisfarne and was to become, in many respects, an east coast equivalent of Iona.

1  *St Mungo*, ed. Iain MacDonald (Floris Books, Edinburgh 1993), pp.23-24
2  ibid. p.24

*chapter nine*

# The Inheritance and the Inheritor

*In Alba in shining purity,*
*having relinquished all happiness,*
*went from us to his mother.*

OLK-MEMORY plays curious tricks on us, and the instincts associated with millennia of paganism are still strong, even in the most sophisticated society. The Western Highlands, in the mid-Seventeenth Century were neither sophisticated nor completely unlettered, but they were able to produce a situation which caused the Protestant Divines of Wester Ross a sudden flutter of alarm and disquiet.

"Under date 5th September, 1656, the Presbytery met at Applecross with a view of rectifying a serious religious misdemeanour. They had ascertained that many of the inhabitants of the surrounding district had been in the habit of practising certain idolatries, and so late as the previous August had, on the island in Loch Maree, offered up a bull as a sacrifice to 'Mourie' whatever that personage may turn out to be."

The object aimed at by these sacrifices may, we think, be ascertained by referring to a subsequent entry in these Records (1678) in which it is stated that a sacrifice of this nature, and in the same locality, was offered for "recovery of Christine MacKenzie, spouse of Hector MacKenzie of Mellon and Gairloch." The Presbytery had also ascertained that in the parishes of Applecross, Lochcarron,

Lochalsh, Kintail, Coulin, Foddarty, Gairloch and Lochbroom, the ignorant population were in the habit – among other idolatrous practices – of sacrificing bulls on "Maurie's appropriate feast day, the 25th of August." [1]

"Maurie" is easily identified. He is none other than Maelrubha, apostle of the Picts of the extreme West and North of Scotland, and of Skye and the Isles. The name Maelrubha means "the red-tonsured one" and invites speculation as to the colour of his hair. In Gaelic, he is known as Sagart Ruadh, "the red priest." Maelrubha, therefore, might well have been what we would regard as a nickname. 27th August is his Scottish feast-day; 21st April is the Irish.

Maelrubha was born in Ireland, on January 3rd in the year 642. His father was an Irish Gael, Elganach MacGarbh, of the Binnigh branch of the great Clan Niall. Not long before his birth, the Clan Binnigh had seized the former Irish Pictish lands in South Tyrone and the days of the Brythonic-speaking Irish as a separate people were by then already numbered. Maelrubha's mother was an Irish Pict, Subtan, the daughter of Sedna, and she was either a niece or more probably a grand-niece of Comgall the Great, founder and first Ab of Bangor in Ulster.

It need not surprise us, therefore, to learn that Maelrubha entered the *muinntir* at Bangor, and trained under the abbots Baithene and Critan. At the age of 29 he left and entered into the 'white martyrdom' of exile in order to evangelise the still untouched stretches of the north-west of Scotland and its Isles. That this vast and rugged land was still unevangelised we learn from the attempt of the Pictish evangelist, Donnan, to interest the Gael, Colmcille, in a joint venture. This he failed to do, for reasons unclear, and Colmcille is said to have warned him against it and prophesied his martyrdom if he persisted in the venture.

Donnan persisted indeed, and was in fact martyred, with fifty-two brethren of his Community, in the refectory adjoining his church on the island of Eigg, on 17th April in the year 617. Frisian pirates were already making sporadic raids along the coast some decades before the arrival of the Scandinavian Vikings.

An ancient account of the martyrdom tells us, "At length, men came to slay them. The cleric was now at the Oifrend (the Eucharist). 'Let us have respite till the Oifrend is ended,' asked Donnan. 'It

99

will be granted,' replied they. Afterwards, the whole company were martyred together."

Maelrubha crossed over to Scotland, warnings notwithstanding, in order to enter into his 'white martyrdom' and to begin his life's great work.

# JouRqeys aqò ɔissioqs

Maelrubha spent his first two years journeying up the west coast of Scotland and is known to have established six foundations which still echo his name. One of them, Cill Mha'ru, is on Eilean an t-Sagairt or 'Island of the priest' near Muckairn, and similarly named is the ancient church site at Arisaig. None of these places are easy to live in, though their beauty is almost painful to the Celtic heart. The beauties of nature, icon of its Creator, surrounded Maelrubha, harsh though the climate was, as often as not.

From Arisaig, Maelrubha sailed north until he found what he was looking for, a site for a permanent base for his Community. He found it at Abhain Crossan Abercrossan, the confluence of the Crossan – and there his built his principal church. The district came to be known as *A Chomraich*, the sanctuary, in which a shedder-of-blood could claim the protection of the Church and be sure of a fair trial. The name is now garbled into the present-day *Applecross*.

From his base at Abercrossan, Maelrubha spent the next half-century evangelising the north-west corner of the Scottish Highlands. His mission included the Isle of Skye and ranged as far afield as Lewis in the Outer Hebrides. Nor was he content to work only in the west. Venturing east as far as the Cromarty Firth and Keith in Banffshire, there is a line of Maelrubha foundations, linking him with the earlier work of his own distant relative, Moluag.

It is important to remember that, although we know nothing of the other members of his Community, Maelrubha was very far from being a solitary hermit, working alone. His mission work was a corporate enterprise, however much he may have been the leader, founder of a *muinntir* and the driving force behind it. It is not improbable that some work, some foundations, are the work of others who acknowledged Maelrubha as their spiritual leader. Indeed this must have been the case with all the great Celtic missionary saints. They were men far too big to be incapable of delegation.

# maelrubha's martyrdom

In old age, in his late seventies, Maelrubha struck north once more. His line of march can be traced from the chapel on Eilean Ma-rui, in Loch Maree, with its healing well-site of the ridiculous if almost endearing "religious misdemeanours" of a thousand years later – to the cell on Innis Ma-rui in Loch Shin, Lairg, thence to the ancient church site at Durness in northern Sutherland, and finally to the *Teampull* at Skail in Strathnaver, Sutherland, where he was martyred at the age of eighty.

Once more the culprits were Frisian pirates who dragged the old man into 'the thickets' and there murdered him. The date was the 17th of April in the year 722. His grave, with its cross-marked stone, is in the ruins of *Teampull*. An ancient document known as *The Feilire of St Angus* and quoted at the head of this chapter, contains a verse which refers both to his 'white martyrdom' as well as his final 'red martyrdom,' and also to his well-known love for his mother, Subtan, from whom he first learned his Christian Faith.

In respect of that Christian Faith, it is the unity of all things – the unity of God, the Saints and the Angels, mortal men and women, the animals, and the earth and sea that is fundamental to the Christian vision as understood by the Celtic believers in the first millennium of the Christian Revelation. The Incarnation of our Lord Jesus Christ is the fulfilment of all the hopes and strivings of humankind. Devotion to the Blessed Trinity lies at the very heart of Celtic Spirituality, for the doctrine of the Blessed Trinity-in-Unity reveals that "God is Love" but also that, at the very heart of the Mystery of the Divine Being, God is also a Love-Affair.

A slightly younger contemporary of Maelrubha was Bede of Jarrow, who was born in the year 673 and died at the age of sixty-two in 735, eleven years after Maelrubha. It is in this south-easterly direction that we must now direct our attentions, for the Celtic tradition and its distinct Spirituality had already made an enduring mark among the Anglo-Saxons in Northumbria and, in the process, it had met, in head-on collision, the spreading power of Rome.

# Celtic Spirituality in Anglo-Saxon Northumbria

Aethelfrith, the king of Bernicia (Northumbria) had resoundingly defeated the British at the battle of Chester. Within a year, however, he was himself defeated and killed in a battle between rival Anglo-Saxon chiefs, and his sons fled northwards, eventually finding refuge among the Scots of Dalriada, where they one and all embraced the Christian Faith.

Bernicia fell to Edwin, king of Deira, whose capital was at York. Edwin was married to a Kentish princess who was a Christian and who brought with her a Roman monk by the name of Paulinus. Paulinus succeeded in converting Edwin to the Christian Faith and, as a consequence of this, Edwin's followers became nominally Christian as well.

Edwin continued Aethelfrith's expansionist policies, and Northumbria briefly extended northwards to the south bank of the Forth. The present name of the Scottish capital, Edinburgh, is but a slight corruption of Edwin's Berg and is of his foundation. Paulinus toiled valiantly, as best he could, teaching the faith and baptising multitudes of the half-taught, but any serious practice of the Faith must have been confined to the court, for Paulinus seems to have been the only Christian cleric there was, apart from a young man, a Northumbrian called James, who was made deacon at what was to prove the very last minute, in 633.

In October of 633, Edwin was defeated and killed by the unlikely and probably uncomfortable alliance of Cadwallon, the British and Christian king of Gwynedd, and Penda, the Anglo-Saxon and pagan king of Mercia. Each had his own reason for putting a stop to Edwin and his activities and the Northumbrian 'empire' quickly fell apart. Edwin's widowed queen fled back to Kent, taking Paulinus with her. The newly ordained deacon, James, was left in charge of what few genuine Christian believers there might remain, while the great mass of the population reverted at once to a paganism which they had never really abandoned.

In the meantime, Cadwallon rampaged about Northumbria and made a particular point of destroying Edwin's former headquarters at Yeavering before returning to Wales.

When the news of Edwin's overthrow reached Aethelfrith's sons in Dalriada, his second son, Oswald, decided to return to Bernicia and claim the kingdom. His elder brother Eanfrith, who had abandoned his Christian Faith as soon as he left Dalriada, had been lured into a trap and killed in 634. In the following year, Oswald returned and was immediately challenged by Cadwallon, who attacked him with a large force at Deniseburn, just north of Hexham.

Oswald, who erected a cross at the site of his headquarters, had chosen his ground with great skill. His back was to the north face of the still-standing Hadrian's wall where it crossed a ridge with a steep-sided north slope. Cadwallon, coming up from the south, was obliged to pass through a gate in the wall at the bottom of the hill and some distance to the west of it, and then, with his forces in some confusion and disorder, wheel almost one hundred and eighty degrees and attack the well-placed Anglo-Saxons up a long, steep slope.

Cadwallon was comprehensively defeated, his army was scattered and he himself was hunted down and finally overtaken and killed when he was trapped at the junction of two rivers in what is now Hexhamshire. Oswald's own position was now secure and he immediately attributed his victory to Divine Providence. There is, however, a sad irony in the fact that popular local history sees Oswald, the good Christian, defeating Cadwallon, the bad pagan. In reality, Cadwallon was a Christian of several generations' standing, coming from that part of Britain that had been Christian for perhaps three or four centuries, and his principle motivation was the ridding of his native Britain of these alien – and pagan – invaders!

Oswald was quite clearly a sincere Christian believer, however. He had spent some time on Iona and it was to Iona that he sent, immediately, for a bishop to found a *muinntir* and set about the conversion, or re-conversion, of Bernicia. The first to arrive departed almost as soon as he arrived. He found the Anglo-Saxons impossible to deal with. He was replaced at once by an Irishman, Aidan, who set about the task of conversion by the simple but costly method of living the Faith he preached with a great gentleness and simplicity. Oswald gave him the isle of Lindisfarne for his headquarters and the site of his *muinntir*. It was to be, as nearly as possible, a clone of Iona, and it was the Celtic spirituality emanating from Lindisfarne that formed the first of the many Anglo-Saxon saints, and which was to leave its mark long after the Celts had gone and the authority, and spirituality, of Rome was established throughout the length and breadth of what was to become England.

# Zhe Conversion of Northumbria

Oswald reigned for nine years before being defeated and killed in battle in 642, at the age of thirty-eight. It is said of him that his last words were a prayer for the souls of his bodyguard who were killed with him. Sixty-two churches were dedicated to him in England, but these were dedications in honour, not indications of his own foundations.

During his reign, he and Aidan worked closely together. Aidan knew nothing, at first, of the Anglo-Saxon language and he and the King would work together, Oswald translating Aidan's preaching and commanding that a cross be set up wherever they had been. It would be difficult to imagine a more impressive demonstration to the people that their King was committed to his Faith and to the propagation of it.

After Oswald's death Aidan supported Oswin, king of Deira, the southern of the two kingdoms of Diera and Bernicia. The two became close friends. Aidan evangelised in the usual Celtic fashion, by establishing small 'families' of believers throughout the countryside, and so enabling the Church to spread organically. He established a school on Lindisfarne and educated young Anglo-Saxon boys (often liberated slaves) for the priesthood.

From Inner Farne, where he was accustomed to spend Lent, Aidan saw Bamburgh, the capital of Bernicia, being burned in 651 by the ever-militant Penda, king of Mercia, and it is claimed that it was the prayers of Aidan that caused the wind to change direction and blow the flames away from the defenders and towards the attackers, thus saving the day. In that same year Oswin was killed by his rival Oswiu, who took the throne and united the kingdoms of Diera and Bernicia. It was this same Oswiu who, twelve years later, was to convene the fateful Synod of Whitby where the Celtic Christian tradition was to be confronted by the Roman in a debate in which the contrast in tone was of far greater significance than the substance.

Aidan died in Bamburgh on 31st of August 651. His *muinntir* on Lindisfarne and the Christian Faith in Northumbria were by now firmly established. Anglo-Saxons the folk might be, but it was the Celtic Spirituality of Ireland, via Iona, that was their Christian inheritance. Its influence would remain for generations to come.

# The Synod of Whitby

King Oswiu had been baptised into the Celtic tradition and might have been its secular champion had it not been for his marriage to a Kentish princess, Eanfleda. She was a Christian according to the Continental, that is to say the Roman tradition, and had as her chaplain a priest who was appropriately named Romanus. All would have been well had not the centuries of isolation of the Celts from the continent caused them to be out of step in the matter of the calculation of the movable, but fundamental, feast of Easter. Every so often the Celts and the Romans were a week adrift from one another, and when the King was trying to celebrate Easter while the Queen was entering upon the austerities of Holy Week, domestic tensions in the palace became unacceptable. This was a matter which cried out for resolution as the two traditions came more and more into contact with each other, all working to a common end.

Oswiu therefore resolved that the thing must be settled, once and for all. He summoned a meeting of both traditions at the monastery for both men and women, presided over by the redoubtable Hilda, who was related to the royal families both of Northumbria and of East Anglia. Hilda's monastery was at Streaneshalch, better known by its later Danish name of Whitby.

The Celtic tradition's delegation included Oswiu himself, and Hilda. But to state its case was Coleman, the present Abbot of Lindisfarne, with a handful of Scots clerics and with Cedd, the Lindisfarne-trained Bishop of Essex, as their interpreter. The Roman tradition was represented by Alchfrid, the Frankish Bishop of the West Saxons, a priest called Agtho, Oswiu's son Alchfrid who had been educated by Wilfred, Abbot of Ripon; Romanus, the Queen's chaplain, James the deacon who had served with Paulinus, and Wilfred himself as their chief spokesman.

Wilfred, born in about 633, was educated on Lindisfarne by Aidan and his successor. He became dissatisfied with its isolation, and with Queen Eanfleda's encouragement, travelled to Rome where he enthusiastically embraced everything Continental, and thereafter seems to have held the tradition in which he had been raised in the liveliest contempt. On his return to Britain he became Abbot of Ripon, where he immediately introduced the Rule of St Benedict and, although he mellowed somewhat in later life, his remarkable and distinguished career was marked by controversies, upsets and even periods of exile when he had exasperated local rulers beyond endurance. In 663 Wilfred was a very clever, highly outspoken young man of thirty.

In brief, the Synod of Whitby, which concluded in 664, settled the matter of Easter according to the Continental method of calculation, already adopted in the south of Ireland. Much more significant, however, was the complete alienation of one tradition from the other, provoked by Wilfred's arrogant and contemptuous attack upon the whole Celtic tradition. Wilfred was a master of clever debate, and Coleman, a gentle, holy man, was no match for him. Bede reports Wilfred's argument very fully and, in terms of its tone, it makes sorry reading.

The effect was to cause Coleman and all the Irish monks to leave Lindisfarne altogether. The work of Celtic-trained clergy, ministering in the South and the Midlands, began to be inhibited and, although the Anglo-Saxon Church, particularly in the North, retained much of the spiritual heritage of the Celts, England, as opposed to Scotland, Wales and Ireland, was henceforth essentially a part of a Continental Church in which the mantle of the former Roman Emperors had descended, almost inevitably, upon the shoulders of the Pope.

1  *A Guide to Wester Ross*, A.C.M. Mitford (Fifth Edition, Northern Times Ltd. Golspie, Sutherland) pp.64-65.

*chapter ten*

# The Forgotten Faith?

AMONG THE MANY traditions concerning Colmcille – or Columba as he is better known – there is one concerning his arrival on the isle of Iona. Iona was chosen because it was already a Holy Island of the druidic faith and, according to this tradition, Columba sought out Oran, the chief druid, and said to him: "Your faith looks forward to the time when the Sun-god shall walk the earth as a man and all the ills of the world shall be healed. I am come to tell you that it has happened! God has walked the earth as a man and his name is Jesus!"

There is no way of knowing either the truth of this tradition or its origins save that there is something about it that rings true. Colmcille, or Columba, came from an Ireland which had been evangelised with great gentleness and with an obvious sensitivity which saw the pagan hope fulfilled in Christ and the best and most true of what had gone before able to be 'baptised' and fulfilled in its turn within the new Faith. And all without bloodshed. There may well have been much about the druidic, pre-Christian religious practice which was completely incompatible with the Faith, but this is always best overcome by the love which casts out fear rather than by confronting fear with an even greater fear.

Here we may discern the first signs of a 'forgotten faith' which is Faith indeed and far removed from the tendency of later centuries (including our own) to condemn the past out of hand and then try to start from scratch, not with an existing, living context, but with an imported one. And all this claiming faith but manifesting – in part at least – as a fear of evil, a lack of respect for the evangelised and their traditions, and with a patronising arrogance all too often taking the place of true compassion.

The example of Paul in Athens was the inspiration of the Celtic evangelists. Faced with the task of preaching to Greek polytheists, he had taken the trouble to find out how their minds worked and what their religion was all about. He also acquainted himself with their literature, and having spotted an altar 'to the unknown god,' he began by telling his audience something about this unknown god who was none other than God the Creator of Heaven and Earth! Paul went on to illustrate his discourse with quotations from the Greek poets. This was not only the approach of sound common sense, it was also the approach which demonstrated a respect and a Christ-like compassion for his hearers and their beliefs. Thus did Patrick and his contemporaries win Ireland to the Faith.

I have heard Paul's preaching to the Athenians described, dismissively, almost contemptuously, as "his least effective piece of evangelism"! The suggestion is here made that there is an element of 'forgotten faith' in this. Not for nothing does Julian of Norwich refer to "our courteous Lord." Gentleness as well as firmness and an heroic courage are both the hallmarks of the Celtic Saints and the key to the Holy Spirit's achievements in and through them.

It has been suggested that had Irish monks encountered the civilisations of Central and South America, rather than the Spanish of a later century, a very different style of conversion might have been effected. By the same token, had the North American Indian met the compassion and courtesy of Celtic spirituality rather than the bleak and uncomprehending pieties of the Reformation, there might have been a happier and less guilt-ridden outcome to that encounter between mutually alien cultures.

# A Certain Restlessness

There is, probably in every generation, a certain restlessness and dissatisfaction with the current order of things, whatever it is, and a desire to 'go deeper' or to 'get behind' overlays and perceived obscurations and to rediscover the Faith in its original purity. This is a healthy dissatisfaction provided it does not become obsessional or fantastic and pursue its own agendas altogether too blindly.

Thus the question is often asked, "What about those other Gospels," the apocryphal books of the New Testament fringe? What might they have to tell us, and what might have been suppressed or deliberately hidden by whoever and for whatever motive? Happily, a study of the texts in question reveals, quite quickly and all too plainly, why the collective mind of the early Church put them to one side and why most of them have half-vanished in their own obscurities.

In much the same way the question is often asked, "What has been lost? What did the Celtic Church have that we do not seem to have, and in what ways did Celtic Christianity differ from that of present-day Rome or the Reformation?"

This is a much more substantial question and more difficult to answer in fairness and with accuracy. Is there such a thing, or was there ever such a thing as 'Celtic Christianity?' The answer is no, there was not. But there was, and is, very much such a thing as a distinctive Celtic Spirituality. It is to this that we must pay attention in this final chapter and, to some extent, we have already begun to do so.

# celtic spirituality

The first and most compelling characteristic of Celtic Spirituality is its orthodoxy. God is almost unfailingly referred to, and addressed, as Trinity-in-Unity. It may be that this came easily to the Celtic mind whose pre-Christian religious pantheon was full of threefold gods and goddesses.

Nevertheless this emphatic and entirely orthodox trinitarianism, experienced as a vibrant, living Reality and not as anything in the least academic, is striking. God is Love, as John tells us, but the paradoxical – and ultimately unfathomable – mystery of the Trinity-in-Unity tells us that, at the very heart of the Mystery, God is also a Love Affair.

The unspoken but implicit recognition that God is both Love and a Love-Affair puts the whole of creation into context, for the context of creation is revealed as a Love-Affair!

Creation is beautiful, beloved and blessed; it is the transfigured image of its Creator. Creation is also all of a piece; there is no artificial separation between the farmer, his cow, his land, the Saints and the Holy Angels. All are part of the one inseparable whole, and the Persons of the Trinity, always understood as Trinity-in-Unity, are intimately involved in the creation at all its levels and with an infinite and unfailing compassion. There is no conceivable separation between 'religion' and 'life.' Indeed human life, transfigured in the Father, the Son and the Holy Spirit, might almost be described as 'religionless,' but such words must be used with some care for they are fraught with all sorts of possibilities of misunderstanding.

The Three-in-One and the Dual Nature of Christ, fully God and fully Man, are mysteries which are ultimately unfathomable. They can only be articulated poetically and they are realities which are experienced and not 'known about.' The Celtic mind is unafraid of mystery and abides within the context of poetry for it comes naturally to the Celts to define themselves in terms of myth rather than in terms of history. History records what actually happened, mythology articulates the perceived meaning of what happened. The two are no more in conflict than science and religion, they simply ask – and endeavour to answer – different questions.

# CREATION, BLESSED AND BEAUTIFUL

Creation is good, and blessed and beautiful. The creation myth in Genesis sees God creating and then seeing that what He had created was good. There is no world-rejection in Celtic spirituality, no hint that the material creation is anything other than blessed. Its beauty is celebrated over and over again, particularly in the writings of Irish monks in the first thousand years of Celtic Christian history. The land, the plant-life, the creatures of wood and field and the bird life are all described with adoration, all participating in the transfigured image of the Creator which is the Celtic vision of creation. As we shall see, a very different, and largely intellectual influence was abroad in the Mediterranean world, which although never consciously embraced by the Church, nevertheless subtly and in some ways quite powerfully influenced it. It was the good fortune of the Celtic lands to have been protected, by distance and by other circumstances, from a number of subtle distortions whose origins were quite alien from either the Hebrew Bible or the Christian Gospel.

A tendency towards creation-rejection has manifested from time to time and within very different traditions. The Puritans of the English Commonwealth prohibited all music and dancing; the only permissible singing was of psalms and hymns. The utterly different tradition of the Counter Reformation encouraged such a holy man as the Cure d'Ars to stamp out all music and dancing in his country parish as "of the devil!" The function of folksong and dance, as an articulation not only of human life but of the very landscape in which a people dwells, was simply not perceived, or if perceived at all, rejected out of hand. By the same token the extreme requirements of "custody of the senses" required of members of religious orders at various times indicates a positive fear of creation as a snare and a delusion rather than joy in it as the transfigured image of its Creator.

The Church in the Celtic lands, protected from any creation-rejection, was also protected from a developing style, a Church's attitude towards itself, which belonged to an essentially urban culture, to the influences consequent upon being officially established, and a developing and somewhat Imperial approach to authority and, to an increasing degree, to power. The arrival of Augustine in Kent in 597 precipitated not a conflict within the one essential Christian Faith, but a conflict of styles and of attitudes. Two very different worlds met; the urban and sophisticated and the rural and essentially primitive.

# αugustine of Canterbury: Success and Failure

According to tradition, Pope Gregory the Great was moved to action by the appearance of two young Anglo-Saxon slaves in the Roman slave-market. Told that these good-looking, flaxen haired lads were Angles, he is reported to have replied: "Angles? They look more like Angels!"

The question of the reconversion of Rome's lost Colony of Britain then began to nag him. The indigenous British Church was nothing if not embattled. The pagan Anglo-Saxons were not yet available for conversion by those to whom they were still the invading enemy and a threat to their very existence. Nevertheless there were said to be a few Christians among the Anglo-Saxons, and the Jutish King of Kent, Ethelbert, was married to a Christian wife. There was therefore a reasonable hope of establishing a toehold among the heathens and, if this could be done, of re-establishing contact with the indigenous British Church and of structuring it back in to the Continental mainstream. Then the task of reconversion could be properly organised and started in earnest.

Gregory chose a Roman monk by the name of Augustine, prior of the monastery of St Andrew in Rome, and sent him off on his long journey to Kent, together with a handful of companions. On their way from Italy, up through France, Augustine's nerve failed him. He turned back, only to be smartly turned round and sent off again by Pope Gregory who gave him clearer instructions and commended him to Etherius, the bishop of Aries, who was Primate of the Church in Gaul. Augustine arrived in Kent in 597, made a good impression on the King, and with Queen Bertha's help was fairly quickly established, with the old Romano-British church of St Martin in Canterbury as his headquarters.

In 601 King Ethelbert was baptised and made the Christian Faith official in his kingdom. In the course of a visit to Aries, Augustine was then consecrated bishop of Canterbury. Later in the same year he was sent the Pallium by Pope Gregory which confirmed him as Archbishop and Primate of Britain. With the Pallium came a welcome reinforcement of clergy with which to establish his diocese.

So far, so good. The prospects were better than he had dared to hope; now it was time to deal with the native British and their long-lost Church. Accordingly, Augustine, now Archbishop and charged by the Pope with the oversight of the whole Church in Britain, encouraged and supported by Ethelbert, summoned the British bishops to meet him, in 603, in order that he might formally receive their submission. It was all very reasonable, all very Continental. It would not have occurred to Augustine that there was any other possible course of action.

A first meeting with British clerics was unsatisfactory. Augustine had been very much on his dignity and had demanded that the British Church adapt its order and customs forthwith to Continental norms. A few weeks later a second meeting was arranged. A delegation of seven British bishops, together with a number of advisers, set out from Bangor Iscoed to meet this new Archbishop of Canterbury. The agenda included such matters as the adoption of the Roman system for the calculation of Easter and their own submission to his authority as papally appointed Archbishop and Primate. How were they to deal with these startling issues honestly and in a truly Christian fashion?

On their way they consulted an anchorite, a known and respected holy man. "If Augustine is a man of God, follow him." This was the answer they got. But how were they to discern if Augustine were truly a man of God? The anchorite said, "If Augustine is meek and lowly of heart it shows that he bears the yoke of Christ himself and offers it to you. But if he is haughty and unbending, then he is not of God, and you should not listen to him." Pressed further, the anchorite continued, "If he rises courteously as you approach, rest assured that he is the servant of Christ and do as he asks. But if he ignores you and does not rise, then, since you are in the majority, do not comply with his demands."

Augustine received his brethren coldly and remained seated. They then accused him of a pride which made nonsense of his claims. The meeting had got off to the worst of all possible starts and ended in total failure. It is easy to blame Augustine, but as one who had once turned back from his mission, he may have been less sure of himself than he cared to admit and thus all the more haughty and unbending in consequence of it. And he was brought up to a different style in a different culture. The British bishops, probably monastic bishops rather than diocesan, might have given an almost rag-tag-and-bobtail impression of themselves to a cleric from the Imperial City. Chalk was meeting cheese and beyond doubt there were ill-chosen words uttered on both sides.

It was to be the very end of the Twelfth Century before the Welsh bishops eventually submitted to the primacy of Canterbury, with the diocese of St David's only coming into line at the beginning of the Thirteenth. Immediately, however, Augustine returned to Canterbury and busied himself with the consolidation of the Church in Ethelbert's realm. He established the monastery of St Peter and St Paul in Canterbury (now known as St Augustine's) and the episcopal sees of both Rochester and of London, then a town of the East Saxons under Ethelbert's overlordship.

Augustine was of great assistance in helping Ethelbert to draft the first written laws for his kingdom and he ordered all ecclesiastical affairs as closely as possible to the Roman model which, needless to say, was the only one he knew. Augustine died on 26th May 604 after a ministry of seven eventful years. We shall now have to consider some of the subtler influences he might have brought with him from the Imperial City. Perhaps the most disturbing relates to a contemporary of Ninian of whom some mention has already been made in Chapter Three.

# The Other Augustine and his Legacy

Almost two and a half centuries before Augustine landed in Kent there was born another by the same name in Tagaste in present day Algeria. This earlier Augustine was a brilliant youth, the child of a devoutly Christian mother and a somewhat nominally Christian father, and was brought up in the Faith but not baptised into it.

At university in Carthage he discarded the Faith altogether and devoted himself at one level to brilliant intellectual pursuits and at another level to sexual delights. By the age of fifteen he had a mistress who was faithful to him for over fifteen years, bearing him a son, Adeodatus, towards the end of their relationship.

Augustine travelled to Italy and lectured in law and rhetoric, meeting a number of influential people and being much exercised about a return to the Christian Faith. In the meantime he had become a Manichee, a follower of a religious philosophy which owed its origins to Zoroastrian dualism and which regarded the spiritual as good and the material as intrinsically evil, thus being absolutely at odds with Christian belief. After much agonising, Augustine was baptised in 386 and dismissed his heartbroken mistress and her son. The child died within the year.

Celibacy of the Clergy was required in the West (but not in the Eastern Church) by a decretal of Pope Siricius in 386, the year of Augustine's baptism. Under the influence of Ambrose, bishop of Milan, he decided to embark upon the monastic life and returned to Africa, where, for a few years, he led a quasi-monastic life with a number of companions. Augustine was ordained priest in 391 and four years later became bishop of Hippo, which diocese he served most faithfully until his death in 430.

Augustine was a prolific scholar, writer and controversialist whose influence upon the Western Church has been profound, and mostly very much to the good. He was, however, a tormented soul and there were flaws in his personality. There was a streak of cruelty in him and, almost certainly unconsciously, guilt about his earlier sexual excesses began to manifest in a rejection of women and a demonisation of sex itself. In his writings, in flagrant denial of Holy Scripture, he explicitly denied that women could possibly be made in the image and likeness of God! He was able to get away with it because of a woman-rejecting and celibacy-exalting mind at the very heart of the Western Church of his day and, indeed, discernible to some degree almost ever since. Nine hundred years later, St Thomas Aquinas was able to denigrate women in almost exactly the same way as Augustine and also, like him, to get away with it!

Augustine developed a very decided doctrine of Original Sin. Taking the myth of Adam and Eve quite literally he taught that

Adam's disobedience (Eve's fault!) has been throughout the ages a sexually transmitted disease, perverting the image of God in mankind. Sex therefore is inherently sinful! The psychological origins of Augustine's stance in these matters is obvious to our present generation, but it was neither obvious nor particularly shocking then to a Western Church whose clergy were in rapid process of separation from the laity and who were required to be celibate willy-nilly. Sex, never an easy thing for mortal men and women to handle, is quite obviously a highly dangerous business for enforced celibates. Women are also a potential snare for any devout cleric who finds celibacy a hard and over the years an increasingly lonely road to follow. As Scripture reminds us, "It is not good for man to be alone."

There has been a tendency in the Christian West to exalt the celibate life over the married as the better and more holy way, thus putting a particular interpretation upon what our Lord said about "those who make themselves eunuchs for the sake of the Kingdom" and failing to understand Paul's remarks on the subject as having been made in the expectation of an imminent Second Coming. Indeed I remember hearing celibacy exalted as the better way for clergy in an Anglican Theological College in 1962, the English Church having lifted the ban on clerical marriage four centuries earlier!

The teachings of Augustine about women and sexuality have never been part of the Church's doctrines but, nevertheless, they have cast a very long shadow over the Church's life and thought ever since. It was, however, a shadow that was not to fall upon the Church in the Celtic lands until the arrival in Kent of that later Augustine in 597.

# Correspondence with pope Gregory

Immediately following upon his consecration as bishop, Augustine wrote a long letter to Pope Gregory asking for guidance in a wide variety of matters. Pope Gregory answered each point carefully, and his replies, recorded for us by Bede, reveal a kindly, pastorally minded soul imbued with a great deal of common sense. Beginning with matters of Church order, finance and liturgy, he moved on to permitted degrees in marriage, the propriety of baptising pregnant women, regulations about dealing with the menstrual cycle in women and then, at considerable length, he answered Augustine's anxious questions about sexual matters as between husband and wife.

Here it becomes quite plain that sexual activity was regarded as a regrettable necessity for the purposes of procreation but probably inherently sinful in that it was so difficult to avoid the enjoyment of it. At all costs it must not be enjoyed because that is desire – lust – and thus, by its very nature, sin. Given this underlying attitude towards sexuality, Gregory's pastoral approach was remarkably gentle and full of common sense, but the subject was nevertheless highly charged with angst. There was no consideration of women in this, everything concerned men, and there was not so much as a hint of understanding that sexual activity between husband and wife might be a supreme expression of tenderness and of self-giving love, or that a loving Creator might have actually intended it to be an enjoyable activity, and for both parties engaging in it.

Here we may discern the influence, if not of the earlier Augustine himself, then of two centuries of compulsory celibacy in what was by now a clerical hierarchy. Desire, which is capable of being both legitimate in love or illegitimate in lust, was demonised altogether. Woman became little more than a sex-object and, as such, a potential danger to celibate clergy. It may be questioned how much of this was truly conscious and how much had become part of a half-unconsciously inherited attitude within the ecclesiastical group mind. The suggestion is here made that, however disordered sexual affairs may or may not have been in the Celtic Christian world, this underlying negative attitude, this *angst*, had probably not filtered all the way up from the Mediterranean to the Celtic lands until it arrived in Kent in 597 in the half-unconscious mind of Augustine, first Archbishop of Canterbury.

Before we can claim a healthier, less shadowed approach to sexuality in the Celtic Church, however, we must endeavour to discern the Celtic attitude to women prior to 597, and for this we are bound to go to the pre-Christian mythology, faithfully recorded by Christian monks from quite early on in the Celtic Christian period.

It is clear that goddess-archetypes were immensely important; some were nice and some were nasty. Warrior Queens abounded and were as free in choosing handsome young men as the Kings were in choosing pretty young women. The Ulster hero Cúchulainn was sent to Scotland to learn the arts of war from a Warrior Queen and the arts of love from her daughter, indicating a certain equality of the sexes. Historically, the Pictish royal succession was through the women and not the men. There is little to go on, but there is nothing to indicate to us an all-pervading angst in the matter of sexuality or a denigration (through fear) of women in the Celtic mind, pre-Christian or Christian.

Might a healthy attitude towards women and an acceptance of sexuality as good, blessed, an expression of love as well as the means of procreation, and a gift to be enjoyed with thanksgiving, be part of "A Forgotten Faith?"

The suggestion is here made that this may well be the case. It is undoubtedly a great deal more consistent with the Biblical tradition.

# Neither an End nor a Beginning

Our concern throughout these pages has been with the Christian Church in these islands prior to the arrival of Augustine of Canterbury in 597. As the people to whom the evangelists ministered were Celts, that five hundred years or so of local church history was of a Celtic Church manifesting an increasingly distinctive Celtic Spirituality. Separation from the Continental mainstream preserved it from a number of disturbing influences and its faith was very much the primitive faith of the earliest centuries of church life and worship. So, at least, we may be entitled to assume from what is available to us from those far-off days.

It is important to be clear that 597 was neither an "end of innocence" nor a "coming of the Christian Faith to England," which latter seemed to represent the political correctness of our pre-war school history books. It was a significant date, but one that came and went. Within the next century, in England at any rate, the Church was unified as to dates of Easter and as to the primacy of Canterbury for the purposes of Church governance. The Celtic spiritual heritage remained, however, and is readily discernible in the Anglo-Saxon saints who were, in their generation, as remarkable and as memorable as the Celts had been in theirs.

It was a slow process, over centuries, that brought the Papacy into fully Imperial style, and then, and to an ever-increasing extent, in competition with the Holy Roman Emperors for an authority which by now was virtually indistinguishable from power. The hierarchy became slowly but steadily more hierarchical and the Church's *magisterium* ever more magisterial. These were the consequences not of failure but of success, and success brings more, and subtler, problems with it than does failure. The ordinary life of the Church, in the provincial dioceses and in the parishes – which were established in England by Theodore of Canterbury (d.690) – carried on much as before and has done so ever since. The various spiritualities: Celtic, Anglo-Saxon, Reformed, Continental and Anglican, are all essentially interwoven within the one Faith.

# By Way of Conclusion

In respect of our quest for 'A Forgotten Faith,' it is important to remember that the Faith is so all-embracing and its implications so bewildering that, at any one time a great deal is likely to have slipped below present awareness under the pressure of other concerns, other facets of the one jewel. A faithful spirituality is always aware of its probable need for corrections, checks and balances and of the benefit of learning from other, and different approaches.

The Celtic Christians of the first half-millennium of our Faith are a standing reminder, not only to our own age but to any age, of some very simple, primitive truths:

1. The Faith is most effectively preached by the living of it. It is by the life of the would-be evangelist that the words given to him become audible and acquire life and meaning.
2. Those who would evangelise must 'do their homework' and learn as profoundly as possible what those to whom they would preach the Gospel actually believe, what motivates their lives and what, in their own tradition, might begin to speak to them of Christ. This is a labour of love and love includes respect for persons and also for their beliefs. It needs to be remembered that knowledge proceeds to understanding, and understanding opens the heart to wisdom and true compassion.
3. Creation is good, beautiful and blessed; the transfigured image of its Creator. Humankind is the Manager, or Steward of God's creation and responsible for it. Creation is humankind's context and men and women are both integral parts of it and dependent upon it.
4. Creation is all of a piece. There is and can never be any separation between Heaven and Earth other than in the disordered heart, mind and will of men and women. The whole context of Heaven and Earth is the Everlasting Love. The whole purpose of the Incarnate Life was the deification of humankind, the making of all things new and the summing up of all things in Christ.

One could go on, but as all these reminders are part and parcel of the one universal Faith they are simply singled out here as particular and primitive strengths of Celtic Spirituality which can be healthy correctives to the attitudes and approaches of a more cluttered, more sophisticated age.

Of all the reminders that our brethren of the first five centuries can give us, the most profound is that of simple trust in the Holy Spirit of God to reveal Christ to the hearts and minds of whoever He calls and to "keep the show on the road" in and through the lives of those whom He has chosen in any circumstances whatsoever, be they the most fair or the most foul, and to manifest the Everlasting Love to every eye open to see it, and any heart and mind willing to think it possible.

# Index

Lightning Source UK Ltd.
Milton Keynes UK
UKOW02f0224291014

240809UK00002B/362/P